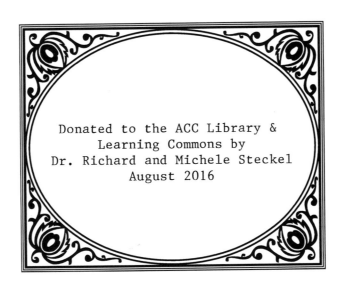

CERAMICS

HOLT, RINEHART AND WINSTON
New York - Chicago - San Francisco
Toronto - London

CERAMICS

Glenn C. Nelson

University of Minnesota, Duluth

PREFACE

I suspect that most of us still recall with pleasure childhood experiences after a summer rain—wading through pools of rain water and feeling the pliant clay squeeze between our toes. For girls, perhaps making mud pies was more the order of the day.

The great interest of recent years in ceramics stems in part, I believe, from such memories, mostly forgotten but subconsciously retained. Certainly the plasticity of clay has made it one of the more exciting mediums with which to work. In its fired state it is one of the most ageless materials. Its three-dimensional qualities plus the effects of glaze, color, and texture make ceramics potentially the richest of all art forms.

Unfortunately ceramics is a rather fickle mistress. While in essence clay is the most elemental of materials, there are many "dos" and "don'ts" involved in working with it. Novice potters have many difficulties with the idiosyncrasies of clay. This book is an effort to develop a reliable guide for the amateur as well as a reference work for the more advanced potter. Ceramics is the most technical of all art forms if the ceramist hopes to achieve a complete understanding of the medium. Unfortunately unless the potter has a good background in ceramics, his potential results are bound to be limited.

Students and other learners will find the illustrations of step-by-step forming methods very useful guides. However, I do not believe that ceramics can be taught solely from the printed page. For this reason the critical aspect of ceramics—design—is left entirely to the studio presentation where it must be resolved in a mutual interaction between the student, the material, and the teacher.

Both the novice potter and the new teacher have equipment problems. Chapter 12 is devoted to this area and the Appendix lists, by geographic area and type of supply, major supply dealers.

The emphasis upon both contemporary and historical ceramics is unusual in a book of this nature; yet it may well be its most important feature. After all, the final potted form is my paramount concern. All technique is subservient to it. Many cultures have produced lasting works of art with a minimum of facilities.

The enthusiasm of the novice potter is, as it is for all human endeavors, the most important ingredient for learning the art of ceramics. I hope that in providing information on techniques and equipment and by illustrating forming methods, I have helped to eliminate some of the initial frustrations of clay-working. The ironic feature of ceramics is that in spite of all this discussion about technique, opening a kiln is much like coming downstairs on Christmas Day—one never knows quite what to expect. For the practicing potter firing may well be one of the more intriguing aspects of ceramics. It gives credence to the old story that the ancient Chinese habitually formed a figurine to be placed on the kiln door to ward off evil spirits. Evil spirits or no, it is my hope that this volume will be of assistance to the pottery student as well as an aid to the many potters who, like myself, are involved with the teaching of ceramics.

G. C. N.

Duluth, Minnesota
February 26, 1960

ACKNOWLEDGMENTS

For their help and encouragement I am grateful to my friends and associates and especially to the many graduate students for whom the original versions of this text were compiled. I am also very grateful for the suggestions received from many fellow potters. Their kindness in supplying the excellent illustrations of their work is most gratifying, and, indeed, these illustrations may well be the most important feature of the book.

To several contemporary foreign potters I am equally grateful for the privilege of showing their works. I am especially indebted to Murray Fieldhouse of England's *Pottery Quarterly*, to Asger Fischer, director of *Den Permanente*, Copenhagen, to Olf Hard of *Form* magazine, Sweden, and to my old friend Olaf Gummerus, director of the Finnish Design Society.

Many art museums have also been most helpful in supplying illustrations from their collections. To my numerous requests for information and reproductions the manufacturers of ceramic equipment have likewise been most cooperative.

The process photographs will be of interest to many students. For his friendly patience and professional skills I am indebted to Ken Moran, who took these photographs.

CONTENTS

ILLUSTRATIONS

CERAMICS

The endless variety of shape is one of the more
desirable qualities of clay. Unfired ceramic vases
by Paul Soldner.*

CHAPTER I

CLAY

Characteristics of Clay

Clay is the most important single material used in ceramics. Potteries first
developed alongside river banks where the action of the stream exposed
clay beds. Until fairly recent times, a close supply of wood for kiln fuel
was also essential. When we think of ceramics, pottery comes to mind as
the major item. Actually, the use of clay and refractories in such forms as
building brick, building and drainage tile, plumbing fixtures, electrical
insulators, and linings for steel and glass furnaces is far more valuable in-
dustrially than is pottery production. In 1958, an estimated 42.3 million
tons of clay were mined in the United States. Since the transportation of
such a quantity of material is quite expensive, the largest number of potteries are in such states as New York, Pennsylvania, and Ohio where there
are good supplies of pottery-type clays. Although there are numerous clay
beds in the Midwest, most deposits are of a shale type and contain numerous iron and alkaline impurities which not only color the clay and lower
its fusing point, but, in general, limit its use to the manufacture of building
brick and drainage tile. However, as it is low priced, we use much of this
kind of clay here at the school in many of our low-fire bodies where color
impurities are not important. In addition, we use several clays mined in
Colorado, Ohio, Kentucky, Georgia, Missouri, and New York.

Seldom can one successfully use a clay just as it is dug from the ground.
Depending upon its origin, clay usually contains varying amounts of par-

* Unless otherwise identified, ceramists represented here are working in the United States.

The experimental textural possibilities of clay are almost limitless. An unglazed dish by William Daley.

tially disintegrated rock, flint pebbles, or sand. If too many foreign objects are present, it hardly pays to bother with the clay. Instead, a new bed should be located. It is an interesting experience to dig and process one's own clay. For the studio potter, it may even be profitable, provided the clay bed is relatively clean and conveniently located. For those teaching crafts in summer camps where time is not at a premium, it is a recommended procedure. The young people usually enjoy the experience, and searching for clay can easily be combined with an afternoon hiking trip.

Commercial clay operations generally employ a power shovel to strip away the overlying earth, exposing the clay bed beneath. In our search for a mere few hundred pounds of clay, we have to rely on the accidents of either man or nature which expose it to our view. In general, these are highway or railroad cuts, river banks, or steep eroded hillsides. There are very few sections of the country, however, in which a workable clay suitable for a low-fire type of pottery cannot be found. If approached properly, most property owners are cooperative. In fact, I once met a farmer who not only gave me permission to prospect for clay, but also advised me of possible locations and then helped me dig and pack the clay. Later, out of curiosity, he visited our workshop to see what sort of pottery could be made from that sticky mud dug near his creek. Most people regard clay as little more than a wet-weather nuisance, but it is this particular quality of clay in which we are interested.

Tests for Clay

1. PLASTICITY OF CLAY is of primary importance, since the success of the potter depends upon the capacity of the wet clay to maintain its shape under the pressure of the hand during the forming process. The fineness of the individual clay particle has much to do with plasticity. The shape of the particle is also a factor. To see this, contrast an extremely plastic montmorillonite-type clay such as bentonite with a kaolinite-type clay which can be classed from average to poor in plasticity. Kaolinite particles average 0.7 microns in diameter and about 0.05 microns in thickness, whereas the thin platelike montmorillonite particles average only 0.05 microns in diameter with a thickness so slight that it is difficult to measure with any accuracy.

The presence of small amounts of organic matter encourages the formation of acids which in turn break down the compounds composing the clay. It is believed that the presence of organic matter in ball clay is responsible for its plasticity. Its chemical composition is relatively similar to that of kaolin, but kaolin is, by comparison, nonplastic or short. The workability of clay can be greatly improved by aging it in a moist state in either crocks or plastic containers. In China it is customary for whole villages to engage in pottery making. Villagers often store clay in pits to be used by the succeeding generation, while they use clay which has been prepared for them by their fathers. According to accounts in old Chinese manuscripts, the Chinese have the same attitudes toward clay that the French, for example, have toward their wine cellars. Incidentally, the slight aroma of an old clay is merely a mark of excellence.

The first *test for plasticity* usually applied to a new clay is to roll out a soft wad of the clay into a shape the size of a lead pencil and then to coil it around one's finger. If no cracks appear, it is good. Even clay which cracks slightly may be doctored up, but if the clay breaks completely open in coiling, usually its particles are too large or there are too many coarse impurities for it to have any value.

Water of plasticity is to some measure connected with plasticity and its amount can be used as a test of plasticity. The smaller the particle size, the greater the amount of water a given weight of clay will absorb. Take, for example, 100 grams of clay and slowly add water to it until it reaches a state of workability. Then weigh it. Usually clays will absorb from 30 to 40 percent of their weight of water, depending upon their plastic qualities.

2. POROSITY is another important quality which a clay must possess. Strange as it may seem, it is possible for a clay to be too plastic, too tightly compacted to allow the water to dry out without cracking it. In this case, it may be combined with a clay less plastic or mixed with a small amount of flint sand or grog. In all experiments with clays or glazes, accurate measurements must be made and records kept if the effort is to have any value. Tiles of a uniform size should be made and the end-firing temperatures exactly noted.

3. VITRIFICATION at the desired temperatures is another test we must give clay. It is necessary for the clay body to develop to the proper point of hardness at the same temperature at which the glaze used will melt to form a glassy coating over the ware. The most accurate test for vitrification is to fire test tiles to the desired temperatures. These should be weighed, then soaked in water overnight. After the surface water has been dried off, the tiles should be weighed again. The gain in weight should be from 5 to 10 percent for earthenware clays but close to 0 for stoneware and porcelain. A simpler test is to tap the vessel. If it has a high clear ring after the glaze fire, the clay body has the proper relationship between refractory and fluxing elements. If the ring has a dull sound, the body was not fired high enough to mature. If the vessel has warped badly or become otherwise deformed, the clay body is of a lower firing type. In either case, additions will have to be made to the clay body to enable it to mature with the glaze. In order to avoid confusion and regrettable accidents in classroom work, all clay bodies and glazes should be adjusted to a limited number of specific firing temperature. Rather than using minerals for this purpose, it is generally preferable to blend two or more clays in order to retain plasticity. Earthenware clays containing fair amounts of iron impurities or alkaline fluxes will lower the firing range in a clay body in the cone 04 to 1 group as will additions of red-iron oxide, nepheline syenite, or talc. Adding feldspar, lime, or bone ash will lower the maturing temperature for higher firing stoneware- or porcelain-type bodies. The use of a high-maturing clay, such as stoneware, fire clay, ball clay, or kaolin, depending upon the plastic or color qualities desired, will raise the vitrifying temperature for low-fire bodies.

SHRINKAGE OF CLAY was mentioned before in connection with the porosity necessary for clay to dry out properly without cracking. Kaolin shrinks from 3 to 10 percent and the ball clays from 5 to 12 percent in the initial drying process. The additional shrinkage which occurs during firing depends, to a considerable extent, upon the end-firing temperature, but it might be roughly estimated at one half of the initial shrinkage. Thus, the total shrinkage is in the neighborhood of from 10 to 15 percent. It is essential that all clay slips used in decorative processes shrink at the same rate as the body or flaking and peeling is apt to result. Because of shrinkage variations, alterations will occasionally have to be made in the glaze formula, depending upon its use on either raw ware or bisque. More will be said on the cooling contractions of glazes in relation to the body in the sections to follow.

PREPARATION OF CLAY is a process which every prospective potter must learn. Although, in general, clays are purchased in a screened and powdered form, there are occasions when it is necessary to use lump clay. In Europe, the lump clay is often left outside to thaw and freeze during the winter, thus improving its plasticity, but we are in too much of a hurry here. For purchased lump clay or clay which the potter has dug himself, this procedure should be followed.

1. Dry out the lump clay completely.
2. Pound the clay with a mallet into a coarse powder.
3. Sift the powdered clay through a ½-inch mesh screen to remove large pebbles, roots, and other impurities.
4. Pour the clay slowly into a bucket, crock, or barrel of water. Use an excess of water.
5. Wait to stir until the clay has naturally soaked up the water.
6. Allow the clay to soak, stirring occasionally until all the lumps disappear. (This may take several days.)
7. Strain the clay through a 14 to 16 mesh sieve. To be strained, the clay must be in a slip (watery) form.
8. If there is too much sand in the slip clay, stir the clay and, after a portion of the sand has settled, decant it into another vessel.
9. Blend in any other clays or materials at this time.
10. Allow the clay to settle, siphon the water off the top, and if you are in a hurry, place the clay in plaster bats. Otherwise, let the excess water evaporate before batting.

Before preparing any amount of new and untried clay, carry out the tests which have been described, since necessary additions are best made when the clay is in the slip state.

Types of Clay

CLAY is essentially a decomposed granite-type rock. It was formed by a process which took millions of years to complete and which is still going on.

Due to the varying conditions under which this breakdown took place, clays are classified into several types.

RESIDUAL CLAYS

Residual clays are those clays which are found in the same position as the parent rock. Their breakdown occurred largely through the constant seepage of ground water through the mass carrying with it CO_2 from the air and organic acids from vegetation. These clay beds contain considerable amounts of unaltered rock so a process of cleaning must take place to get the pure clay.

KAOLIN ($Al_2O_3 \cdot 2\,Si\,O_2 \cdot 2\,H_2O$) is probably the most common and valuable of the residual clays. It takes its name from a Chinese term meaning "high ridge." Kaolin or "China clay" was first used in ceramics by the Chinese. Important deposits are also found in Cornwall, England; Zettlitz, Germany; and Karlsbad, Czechoslovakia. We are fortunate to have several good deposits in the United States, the chief of which are located in North Carolina. Other residual kaolin mines are found in Pennsylvania and Washington. Kaolin fires white in color and is used in combination with flint, feldspar, and ball clay to form high-fire white-ware and porcelain bodies. It has the disadvantage of not being very plastic, a factor which is less important in mechanically formed industrial ware than in hand-thrown pieces.

SEDIMENTARY CLAYS

Sedimentary clays are clays formed from particles which were washed down from high rock formations and settled in the bottoms of lakes and lagoons. The most important of these are the *sedimentary kaolins* and the *ball clays* ($Al_2O_3 \cdot 2\,Si\,O_2 \cdot 2\,H_2O$). Kaolin deposits of the sedimentary type are found in South Carolina, Georgia, and Florida. Since the original particle size was small enough to become water-borne, these kaolins are finer and more plastic than the residual type. This is especially true of the Florida deposits. Ball clays were originally deposited in swamps and contain considerable organic matter. Though of a gray color in the raw state, ball clays burn out in firing to a white or near-white; there is, however, considerable shrinkage. Because of the decomposing action of the vegetable matter with which it was deposited, ball clays have a finer particle size and a greater plasticity than most other clays. They are commonly used as an addition to other, less plastic clays to facilitate the forming process.

A stoneware double bottle form with an iron-ash glaze and a scratched design. Toshiko Takaezu.

Photo by Raymond D. Sato, Honolulu Academy of Arts

FIRECLAYS are found in many sections of the lower Great Lakes area, Colorado, and the Pacific coast states. Like kaolin and the ball clays they are composed largely of alumina and silica, but they have slightly larger amounts of iron impurities and fluxes such as magnesia, potash, and soda. Since fireclays generally fire to a gray color and mature between 2500° and 2700° F, they are little used by the commercial potteries which prefer a white body and a lower firing temperature. Studio potteries, however, which are less concerned with white dinnerware, often use the more plastic fireclays in compounded stoneware bodies firing from 2300° to 2400° F. Commercial uses for fireclay are largely of the refractory type (kiln bricks, kiln furniture, glass ovens, crucibles, and heat-treating furnaces).

STONEWARE CLAYS are commonly found in the territory stretching east from Missouri to New York and in the Pacific coast area. In general, they are similar to the fireclays except that they contain a greater amount of flux in the form of feldspar. By itself feldspar cannot be classed as a flux but it contains a fair amount of the alkaline fluxes (potash, soda, or lime, usually in combination). Stoneware clays in general fire to a light gray color and mature between cones 8 to 10 (2300° to 2380° F). As a group, the stoneware clays are the most useful clays for the studio potter. They usually take their individual names from the mine or locality in which they are produced, such as Jordan or Monmouth, and vary slightly

Sugar bowl with wax-resist decoration, reduced stoneware body. Warren and Alix Mackenzie.

in color, workability, and firing range. Stoneware bodies, however, are seldom compounded from a single clay but rather from several clays or ingredients which combine to form the desirable characteristics of plasticity, color, and the correct firing temperature.

EARTHENWARE CLAYS in general contain too many fluxes to serve as refractory clays and too many iron impurities for use as whiteware bodies. These clays are distributed quite widely throughout the Middle West, the Northeast, and the West Coast state of Washington. Most are formed by the weathering of local rock formations but some are glacial in origin. Earthenware clays are primarily used in the manufacture of bricks and industrial tiles since a fairly strong bond is formed at moderate temperatures (below 2000° F). All of the pottery produced in the Orient prior to about A.D. 250 was made from this red- or cream-colored earthenware. At approximately this date the first protoporcelain evolved. However, earthenware pottery has been the rule in the Western world until fairly recent times. The Oriental secret of porcelain was not duplicated in Europe until 1710. The New World cultures never developed a stoneware or porcelain body; neither did they use a potter's wheel or develop a true glaze. Nevertheless, these various cultures produced a very significant

CLAY BODIES - 11

body or work, proving again that technical knowledge plays a minor role in creating an art form.

SPECIAL CLAYS

There are several other clays of an unusual nature which do not fit into the above categories.

SLIP CLAYS are usually of a glacial origin and are found in a limited number of places, chiefly New York and Michigan. Albany slip from New York is perhaps the best known of the slip clays. It is a natural clay but functions as a glaze and is primarily used as a brown-black glaze on stoneware jars and electric insulators firing at cone 8 or above (2300° F). (See slip glazes, p. 23.)

BENTONITE is formed from a decomposed volcanic glass or ash. Colorado is the chief producer but there are other deposits in the South and West. Bentonite is very plastic because of its extremely small particle size. It is used to increase the plasticity of other clays and the adhesiveness of glazes. About one part of bentonite is usually equal to about five parts of ball clay as a plasticizer.

Clay Bodies*

EARTHENWARE is usually made from a natural clay, fired to some temperature between cone 08 and cone 2 (1740° to 2130° F), most of it in the neighborhood of cone 04. The body is nonvitreous and will not hold a liquid unless glazed. Its color is usually buff or red, often quite dark. For this reason it is often covered with a white slip or "engobe" before glazes are applied. Leaving it partly textured, however, often effects a pleasing contrast to the smooth glazed areas.

STONEWARE may be made from natural clay or from a prepared body containing a high percentage of alumina and silica. It is fired at a higher temperature, usually cone 8 (2300° F), and as a result is hard and vitreous, able to hold water even when unglazed. Not all clays (natural) can be used for stoneware, for many of them, especially the red ones, would melt and deform at stoneware temperatures. The fired stoneware body usually has a gray color which is due to the presence of small iron impurities. This

* See also "Clay Bodies" in the Appendix.

The busy over-all design on these stoneware pieces does not obscure the simplicity of their form. The dish is 21 inches in diameter. J. T. Abernathy.

body color is the only difference between it and the low-fire porcelains.

PORCELAIN requires the highest fire of all pottery wares. It is always made from a specially prepared body composed of kaolin, ball clay, feldspar, and flint. Since this mixture is not very plastic, it requires more skill to work and aging is almost a necessity.

There is a slight difference of opinion between Oriental and Western definitions of porcelain. By European standards it must be white, completely vitrified, and translucent in the thin areas. The Chinese agree that porcelain should be vitrified and should ring sharply when struck, but they feel that translucency is not necessary and they will accept bodies with a slight gray color. The gray color is due, in part possibly, to the use of a gray body or iron oxide to color a white body when a celadon glaze was applied. By so doing, they obtained a better quality color.

The temperature ranges of porcelain are from cone 8 to cone 16 (2300° to 2670° F). The only dinnerware porcelain presently made in the cone-16 range comes from Copenhagen. Until fairly recent times, the kilns there were still fired with wood in the true Oriental fashion, which was quite an undertaking. Today wood kilns are rather an oddity as gas or fuel oil is used in the larger installations.

A word might be said concerning the term "chinaware," which is applied to a majority of the commercially produced dinnerware of our time. It is rather loosely used to describe a whiteware body which is often semi-vitreous and is fired at temperatures much higher than for earthenware but generally lower than for most porcelains (2200° to 2280° F). Since this ware is all cast or jiggered, plasticity is of secondary importance. Chinaware, or "whiteware," is a compounded body like porcelain but with fluxes added which bring down the firing temperatures and automatically, at the same time, the costs of production. "Bone china" is an example of such a body. Here the flux used is bone ash, made from the calcinated bones of animals. Many whiteware bodies are compounded very expertly and serve their purpose well. Restaurant china, which has excellent durability, is an example. It is regrettable that the producers do not put as much skill into the design as they do into the production and engineering of such ware.

Unlike most pieces illustrated here, this handsome bottle of groggy dark clay is hand built. Karl Martz. (Photo Indiana University Photo Lab.)

CHAPTER 2

CERAMIC GLAZES

Purpose and Definition

THE PURPOSE OF A GLAZE is first to render the vessel waterproof and secondly to enhance its esthetic appeal. Before glazes were discovered, primitive man coated his porous ware with animal fats and plant resins. For decorative effects he was limited to incising or stamping the surface of the clay pot or to coating it with a clay of a contrasting color. Perhaps as much as any other factor, the development of glazes, rich in color and with pleasing tactile qualities, has enabled ceramics to develop into an art form.

THE FIRST GLAZE was, of course, an accident. There are many guesses as to how it was first discovered. The making of glass, the glazing of pottery, and the smelting of metals are linked together since they all depend upon a fairly efficient kiln or furnace, and discoveries in one field were apt to lead to advances in the others. The Egyptians are known to have made glass beads and other small objects of glass at a very early period. The discovery of glass no doubt occurred when an extremely hot fire was built over sand containing considerable amounts of alkalai. The first Egyptian glazed objects are small figurines of steatite (a dense form of talc which was carved rather than modeled), dating from the fifth millenium B.C. Tiles covered with an alkaline green glaze were found in the tomb of King Mena (ca. 3300 B.C.). These are the oldest accurately dated glazed objects. Glass beads have also been found in sites of the Indian Indus Valley cultures dating from this era. These may have been traded items or a local discovery. At about 1000 B.C., the use of lead was added to that of the alkaline earths as a fluxing agent. Its use became widespread in the Middle

Stoneware bowl showing decorative use of two contrasting glazes. Maija Grotell.

East but did not reach Europe until Roman times. Lead glazes were also used in China at an early date. While the oldest glazes are attributed to Egypt, this does not necessarily mean that its discovery spread from there to China. Because of the distance involved and the early date (approximately 3000 B.C.) it is likely that the use of a glaze was a local innovation. As mentioned earlier, the discovery of stoneware and porcelain-type bodies and glazes at about A.D. 250 can be attributed without question to the Chinese. The potter's wheel seems to have been invented in the Uranian Highlands, a territory which was later to become Persia. After its discovery in about 4000 B.C., it spread throughout the Middle East and was in common use after 3000 to 2500 B.C.

WHAT IS A GLAZE? Before we go into various types of glazes and materials, we should define a glaze as clearly as possible. A glaze is a continuous layer of glass, or glassy crystals, on the surface of a ceramic body. The glaze is usually applied as a suspension of the glaze-forming ingredients in water, which dry on the surface of the piece in a layer. Upon firing, the ingredients react and melt to form a thin layer of glass. The major difference between a glass and a glaze is the presence of alumina (Al_2O_3). Glass has a very small percentage of alumina or none at all, whereas it is an important ingredient in glazes, increasing in quantity in the higher fired glazes. Most glazes are fired at much higher temperatures than glass and the addition of alumina enables them to take the higher heat without running excessively. Clays also have large quantities of alumina. Alumina combines with the silica in both the glaze and the body to form crystalline structures (mullite) much harder and tougher than can be obtained by the silica and flux alone.

Low-fire Glazes

(See section in Appendix for specific formulas of the glaze types briefly described below.)

LEAD GLAZES comprise the largest group of low-fire glazes, firing from cones 016 to 02. The group takes its name from the flux used, oxides of white or red lead. Lead is a very active flux, melting at a relatively low temperature, flowing uniformly, and giving a bright, glossy surface. Used alone, it may comprise up to 50 percent of the glaze batch but it is often combined with other fluxes. It is a common practice to use more than one flux, since each one has slightly different qualities, and in combination they tend to encourage a lower melting point and a more complete and intimate reaction than can be obtained from a single flux. Lead has the disadvantage of being very poisonous and care should be taken to avoid breathing the dust or getting particles in the mouth. For this reason, lead is often converted into the nontoxic silicate form by fritting. Vessels glazed with lead should not be used to store liquids containing large percentages of acid fruit juices. Lead glazes fired in gas kilns using manufactured gas will often blister unless the muffles are kept in reasonably good condition. The blistering is caused by the sulphur contained in all manufactured gas. Natural gas or propane will not cause these defects.

ALKALINE GLAZES have a similar firing range to the lead type (cones 016 to 02) and use the alkaline-type fluxes like borax, colemanite, and soda ash. Alkaline fluxes allow for certain color effects, particularly the turquoise-blues which lead glazes cannot produce. The alkaline fluxes, because of their extreme solubility, should never be used on raw ware. The extreme expansions and contractions that alkaline compounds undergo during firing and cooling will cause the body to crack.

A very soft bisque should not be glazed, as it will absorb a portion of the flux, leaving an incomplete and usually a rough textured glaze upon firing. Because of their solubility and their tendency to get lumpy in the glaze solution, these alkaline compounds (like borax) are often fritted into the nonsoluble silicate form. In general the alkaline glazes have a smooth glossy surface similar to the lead group.

High-fire Glazes

PORCELAIN and STONEWARE GLAZES differ from those previously mentioned in several ways. Chief among these is the higher firing temperatures which vary from cone 8 to 16 (2300° to 2670° F). At these temperatures, fluxes such as lead and borax would completely volatilize, but before evaporating, the glaze would run off the ware onto the floor of the kiln. Porcelain glazes are made primarily of kaolin and flint with fluxes of feldspar and limestone (whiting). As such, they are similar to the body composition with which the glaze forms a very close bond. They do not lie on the surface of the clay as the earthenware glazes do. In a microscopic section, the line of junction between glaze and body cannot be detected since the crystals interlock (usually creating a mullite formation). Porcelain glazes are hard (they cannot be scratched by steel) and resistant to most acids, with the exception of hydrofluoric, phosphoric and very hot sulphuric acids. The surfaces may be either smooth or mat. However, they never develop the extreme shine of the low-fire glazes.

Special Glaze Types

FRIT GLAZES are not different chemically from the two low-fire types mentioned before, but rather have undergone a process which renders the raw-glaze materials either nontoxic or nonsoluble. Lead or alkaline fluxes (borax or soda ash) are melted in a frit kiln with silica, or silica and a small amount of alumina. When the glaze becomes liquid, a plug is pulled in the bottom of the frit furnace and the melt discharges into a container filled with water. The fractured glaze particles are then ground to the necessary fineness. Small amounts may be made in the studio using a crucible. The greatest disadvantage is the long grinding time necessary to ball mill it to an adequate fineness; it generally takes 15 to 20 hours.

Many different types of frit glazes are on the market. Not only must the nontoxic or nonsoluble element be taken care of in the frit composition, but the firing range, color possibilities, and expansion factors must be calculated as well. A frit glaze is seldom a complete glaze for several reasons. Since it is usually colorless, opacifiers or colorants have to be added later. The frit has little adherence quality so a small amount of a plastic clay or bentonite is usually necessary. Adjustments for firing ranges likewise have to be made. Frits have a great use commercially where large amounts of standard glazes are used. For the studio potter whose approach is more experimental, glaze frits have a more specific than general use.

Stoneware bottle with the body color breaking through a viscous glaze and a pressed and incised decoration. Marie Woo.

CRACKLE GLAZES are really not a separate type of glaze but merely the result of tensions developed when a glaze and a body expand and contract at different rates. In most glazes, save perhaps the mats, a crackle can be made to develop in the glaze. The simplest way is to substitute similar acting fluxes for others having a different contraction rate. Of course, the reverse is true if a noncrackling glaze is desired. This information can be found in the more complete books on ceramics which give the coefficients of expansion for the common ceramic compounds (see Appendix). A crackle is a network of fine cracks on the surface of a glaze. There is no purpose to using a crackle glaze on other than a light body. To strengthen the effect, coloring oxides or strong black tea is often applied. The Chinese were able to achieve, by successive firings, a network of both large and fine crackles, each stained with a different coloring oxide. A crackle in the glaze can be an interesting decorative device. However, it is more practical on the vitreous stoneware or porcelain body. A crackle on the more porous earthenware body will allow the liquids to seep through and make it unsatisfactory for food purposes.

MAT GLAZES are formed either by adding an excess of alumina or by substituting barium carbonate for some of the flux in the glaze. Therefore, they are usually called either alumina mats or barium mats. A mat glaze should not be confused with a thin, rough, or underfired glaze. It should be smooth to the touch but should have no gloss. The mat effects sometimes observed on underfired glaze are due to incompletely dissolved particles, whereas a true mat develops a different surface crystalline structure. A longer-than-usual cooling time will encourage the formation of mat textures. To test for a true mat cool the glaze quickly to see it if will develop a shine. A mat surface caused by the incomplete fusion of particles will continue to have a mat surface regardless of the cooling time. This type of mat surface is generally a bit rough to the touch, lacking the silky smoothness of the true mat. Mats can be calculated for all temperatures. I particularly like them in the low-fired brackets since typical lead and borax glazes are so shiny that their glare tends to kill all decoration and form.

REDUCTION GLAZES are a type of glaze which develop their particular color characteristics only if fired in a kiln capable of maintaining a reducing atmosphere during certain portions of the firing cycle. The normal kiln firing is an oxidizing fire, especially in a kiln with a good muffle. An electric kiln always has an oxidizing fire since there is nothing in the kiln atmosphere to consume the oxygen, which is always present. To reduce the atmosphere in a gas or oil kiln, the burners and air intake are so regulated as to get an incomplete combustion which releases carbon into the kiln interior. Some of the top muffles will have to be removed in a muffle kiln to allow the combustion gases to enter the kiln chamber. Carbon has a great affinity for oxygen and will steal it from the iron and copper-coloring oxides in the glaze. It was in this manner that the Chinese produced their famous *sang-de-boeuf* (copper reds) and celadons. When either copper or iron oxide is deprived of its oxygen, it remains suspended in the glaze as the pure colloidal metal. Thus the normal green copper glaze becomes a beautiful ruby red with occasional blue or purple tints. The iron oxide in turn loses its usual brownish-red tone and takes on a variety of soft gray-green hues. Because of its likeness to jade, which has religious symbolism for the Chinese, celadons of remarkable quality were developed. In addition to controlling the air intake, the Chinese helped the reduction along by inserting fat pine splinters into the kiln chamber. Today moth balls can be inserted through the peep hole; they are just as effective. The usual reduction fire starts out with an oxidizing fire, and reduction does not begin until the first elements of the glaze start to melt. After the reduction fire has been used at various intervals, an oxidizing fire is used to finish the cycle. Reduction by regulating the air intake always causes a temperature drop so it has to be done intermittently. A so-called *artificial reduction* can be achieved by using a small amount of carborundum (about ½ of 1 percent) in the glaze. The effects are a little different as the color is concentrated in little spots around the silicon carbide particles. But it has the advantage that it can be used in an electric kiln. The firing range of reduction glazes are quite wide, from cone 08 up into the porcelain range.

CRYSTALLINE GLAZES are of two types: One has rather large crystal clusters embedded in or on the surface of the glaze; the second type, also called *adventurine*, has single crystals, often small, which catch and reflect

Stoneware bowl with a copper-red reduction glaze and a Tenmoku brushed decoration. Toshiko Takaezu. Collection Mr. and Mrs. Robert Lee, Honolulu, Hawaii.

Photo by Raymond D. Sato, Honolulu Academy of Arts

the light. These are an interesting group of glazes technically, but they are a bit flashy and were formerly more popular than they are today. The crystalline formation is encouraged by RO additions of zinc and iron, or by titanium (rutile). Borax and soda may also be used, but not lead. Possible firing ranges are wide and, as with mat formations, the rate of cooling is important. In order to allow the crystals to develop properly, the temperature of the kiln should be allowed to drop only about 100 degrees and then held at this level for several hours before slowly cooling off. Crystalline glazes tend to be a bit runny so thin sheets of insulating brick should be placed under the ware.

BRISTOL GLAZES are very similar in most respects to the typical porcelain glaze, except that a relatively large amount of zinc oxide is added. In most cases this tends to lower the melting point and to add a certain opacity to the glaze. Most Bristols fall into the cone 5 to 9 range although formulas have been successfully developed from cones 3 to 14. The most common use of the Bristol glaze is for architectural tile and bricks. Since a large amount of clay is used, the ware is generally given a single fire and there is no problem of shrinkage. However, by calcining part of the clay, the glaze can be fitted to double firings. The commercial single fire usually takes 50-60 hours because of the thickness of the ware being fired but also because, in part, of the extremely viscous nature of the Bristol glaze. It is this quality of the glaze which makes it valuable to the studio potter. Interesting effects may be achieved by using the Bristol glaze over a more fluid glaze which breaks through in spots. A perfect glaze coating must be developed during the glazing operation because the viscosity of the glaze prevents any cracks that may occur from healing. Moreover, the edges of the cracks will pull further apart and bead up. In general, the Bristol glazes are shiny but they can be matted by increasing the amount of calcia while reducing the silica content.

LUSTER GLAZES give a thin metallic coating. This coating is achieved by applying over a fired glaze a solution of pine resin, bismuth nitrate, and a metallic salt dissolved in oil of lavender. This is fired at a low red heat, sufficient to fuse the metal and burn off the resin, but lower than the melting point of the original glaze. A variety of reds, yellows, browns, and silvery-white lusters as well as nacreous and iridescent sheens are possible. The metals normally used are lead and zinc acetates; copper, manganese, and cobalt sulfates; uranium nitrate, and silver and gold compounds. Bismuth is generally but not always used as a flux. Until A.D. 1529, bismuth was thought to be an impure form of silver and therefore the silver mentioned in old records probably was a silver-bismuth compound.

Usually the luster is not an over-all coating but rather it is applied in the form of a design in conjunction with colored slips or stains. This is especially true of Islamic art, which, because of religious edicts against representational painting, developed an unusual type of intricate and interlocking decorative motif. It is supposed that lusterware was discovered first in Egypt. However, it received its greatest development in Persia during the ninth to the fourteenth centuries. With the Moslem conquests, it spread across North Africa to Spain. Finally, in the early sixteenth century, the techniques passed to Italy where luster decoration became quite popular during the Renaissance. The Italian output, although considerable, never reached the quality of the Hispano-Moresque ware, partly because the Italians tended to paint pictures on the ware, imitating the popular painters of the day. After the expulsion of the Moors from Spain in 1610, the quality of the Spanish work declined. While potters in many countries have since worked in lusterware, they have never approached the quality and the integration between design and form found in either the Persian or the Hispano-Moresque ware. (See "Colorants for Glazes and Decoration" for further information on lusters.)

SALT GLAZES are seldom employed today, although from the twelfth to the mid-nineteenth century such glazes were common in Europe and in Colonial America. At present, salt glazes are largely limited to stoneware crocks, glazed sewer pipe, hollow building brick, or similar products. The procedure is a simple one. The ware in the kiln is fired to its body-maturing temperature at which time common salt (sodium chloride) is thrown into the firebox or through ports entering the kiln chamber. The sodium combines with the silica in the clay to form a glassy silicate. Fine sand is often added to the clay to form a better glaze coating. By reducing conditions (incomplete combustion to introduce carbon into the kiln atmosphere) buff or red clays can be glazed either brown or black. Other colors can be obtained only by using colored slips or body stains. The disadvantage of the salt glaze, other than its limited color effects, is that it coats the entire interior of the kiln. This generally renders the kiln unsuitable for other types of glaze firing. The firing range of salt glazes is wide, from cones 02 to 12, but most common firings are from cones 3 to 8.

SLIP GLAZES are made from raw natural clays which contain sufficient fluxes to function as glazes without further preparation except washing and sieving. In actual practice, additions are often made to enable the slip glaze to fit the body or to modify the maturing temperature. But in general these changes are minor ones. The so-called "black varnish" of the Greeks was similar in some respects to a slip glaze except that both its firing range and durability was much lower than our typical slip glazes. Had the Greeks been interested in decorating their ceramics with other than linear pictorial representations, they doubtless would have developed a true glaze, since the Minoans, of whom they were, in part, cultural descendants, had developed glazes more than a thousand years earlier.

Slip glazes were commonly used by the early American stoneware potteries which produced such utilitarian objects as storage crocks, bowls, mugs, and pitchers. Today, one of the major uses of a slip clay mined near Albany, New York, is for glazing electrical insulators with that familiar brown-black color. Other slip clays are found in the vicinity of Rockland and Escanaba, Michigan, Wrenshall, Minnesota, and doubtless many other areas. They fire in a range from cone 6 to 10. Slip-clay fluxes are generally the alkaline earth compounds plus iron oxide in varying amounts. The iron oxide serves, also, to give a color ranging from tan to a dark brown.

The addition of 2 percent of cobalt to Albany slip will give a beautiful semigloss jet black. Wrenshall slip at cone 10 fires out to a pale yellow with the peculiar streaked effect characteristic of rutile. A word of caution: Inasmuch as slip clays are generally mined in small pits, their composition will vary slightly. Each new shipment of material should be tested before being used in quantity. Some Albany slip I have used has been so lacking in the usual brown colorant that the resulting glaze was a pale semitransparent tan.

I feel that studio potters should pay more attention to this group of glazes. Slip clays are easy to apply, adhere well, and fire with few, if any, defects. The composition, chemically, is most durable and since additions are few, much time can be saved in glaze preparation.

Using a rib to pull up a large cylinder, Peter
Voulkos may be fashioning a huge bowl or a unit
for one of his large ceramic sculptural pieces.

CHAPTER 3

FORMING METHODS

On the pages to follow there are numerous illustrations of various clay-
working techniques. The throwing shots are presented as a method and
not necessarily as "the way". Depending upon training and in part upon
physical characteristics each potter will throw in a slightly different
manner.

Most of the emphasis is placed upon throwing on the wheel since other
methods such as the coil or slab present more of a challenge of design than
of construction. Owing to lack of space, mold making, slip casting, jiggering, and other reproductive methods of pottery are not illustrated. The
problems of forming, decorating, and glazing are sufficient for the beginning student. All too often the novice rushes off to slip cast a form which
is essentially ugly and ill-formed. The feeling for a clay form comes only
from working with clay, not from working with plaster or line drawings.

A word of caution about throwing:
1. The clay must be perfectly wedged; it should have no bubbles or
   lumps.
2. It must also be neither too soft nor too hard.
3. The ball should not be opened until it is perfectly centered.
4. Throwing tall and perfectly straight cylinders is the best practice.
   Cut them open to check evenness. When you can get cylinders up
   to 14 inches or so, you are ready to begin to make teapots and other
   objects.

Throwing on the Wheel

CENTERING

1. The clay ball is placed on a freshly moistened bat.
2. While the wheel is turning, the right hand forces the clay down.
3. With the elbows braced at the sides, the hands center the clay.
4. When the clay has been centered perfectly, the thumbs open the ball.
5. Pressing the hands downwards and outwards, open the ball into a thick bowl shape.

3

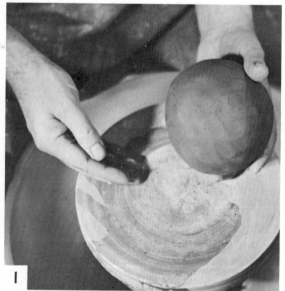

1

4

2

5

THE BOWL SHAPE

From the basic clay form thrown on the opposite page any number of shapes may be made. The bowl presents the fewest problems. The opened ball must be perfectly centered. Throwing should be done quickly lest the clay become too wet. The clay should not be pulled too thin where it flares up from the bat. The concave form must be maintained as any flatness of the curve will cause the piece to sag. Any unevenness in the outer rim may be trimmed with a needle. Moisten the rim and use a soft leather to finish it.

THE CYLINDER

1. The low cylinder must be perfectly centered.
2. Whenever possible, join the hands for better control.
3. If the top is uneven, cut it off with a needle.
4. The walls may be thickened and pulled up slightly by necking.
5. Even pressure forces the clay wall upward.

THE BOTTLE FORM

1. The cylinder shown on the opposite page is flared out by pressure from the inside.
2. The top is necked in and thickened.
3. Then the top is pulled up and thinned out.
4. This process is repeated until the desired shape or height is reached.
5. Finally, the lip is finished with a soft leather.

Trimming the Bowl

1. While the bowl is on the bat, excess clay can be trimmed away.
2. An old hacksaw blade (with its teeth ground off) cuts off the bowl from the bat.
3. Turn the bowl upside down. While it is held in place by soft clay lumps, the excess clay can be trimmed away.
4. The center section is cut out.
5. Making a good foot rim is the final touch to any pot.

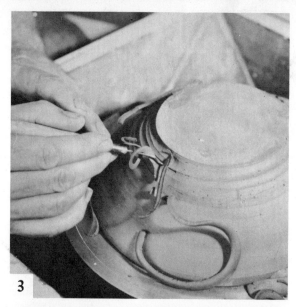

3

1

4

2

5

Trimming the Bottle

The foot is difficult to trim conveniently unless the bottle has a large and stable rim. If the object is small, a wide-mouthed glass jar, centered on the wheel head and held in place with clay lumps, can serve as a turning chuck. For trimming larger pieces, keep in the studio several plaster cylinders of assorted sizes which will fit the wheel heads. With such equipment on hand, trimming the foot of a long-necked bottle or jar is a simple operation.

Drying Problems

After trimming, place the bowls and other objects on a flat shelf in an *upside-down* position, if possible, to equalize the drying rates. Before placing the objects on the drying shelf, wrap the handles of pitchers and similar objects with damp paper towels. If the handles dry first, they will crack off when the drying shrinkage takes place in the body proper.

Production Throwing

A removable bat on the wheel head is usually necessary if one is throwing large objects which will deform seriously when cut and lifted off. Such a bat is also convenient for beginning students who habitually get their clay too wet, but for the experienced potter, who is throwing the smaller objects which are the mainstay of his sales, a plaster bat is a nuisance. The photos below show the throwing of a set of cups. Each is measured for size and trimmed on the wheel head. When cut off with a twisted copper wire, the cups may be easily lifted off to dry. The wheel should be turning slowly while the foot is cut off.

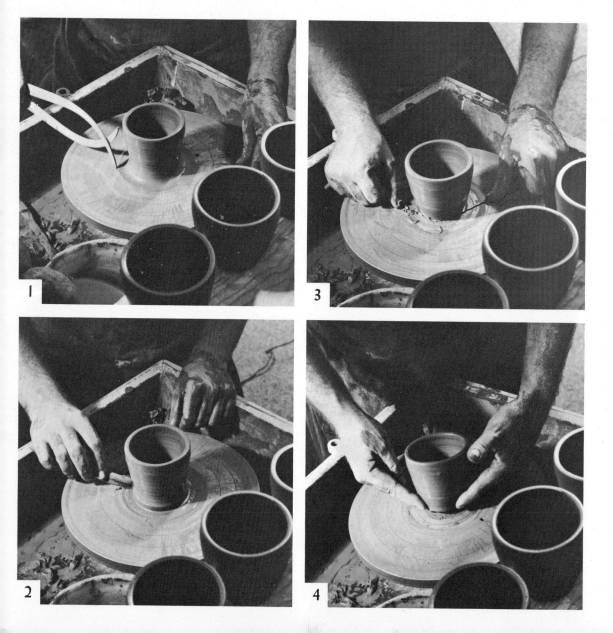

Beverage set with a wax-resist decoration; iron and cobalt oxides have been brushed over the glaze. Nan and James McKinnell.

The Pitcher

1. The lip is shaped from the soft clay.
2. The handle is pulled from a lump of stiff clay.
3. Formed with plenty of water, the handle takes the natural shape of the fingers.
4. The handle is attached as soon as the pitcher is firm enough to work with.
5. The finger marks where the handle is joined make a natural decoration.

3

1

4

2

5

The Tea Set

The tea set is one of the more interesting projects for the potter, both in design and in technique. Within the limits dictated by function, an infinite variety of form is possible.

The tea service by Donald E. Frith (left) features a raffia handle of an unusual design.

The stoneware tea set by Nan and James McKinnell (below) is decorated with an off-white speckled reduction glaze and sgraffito design.

The Teapot

The teapot presents a number of interesting problems to the potter. The relationship designwise between the various parts must be envisaged before throwing begins. The lid must be so flanged that it will not fall out. The handle should balance well and should be designed so that it will not become too hot. The spout must pour properly and its strainer should be large enough and located low enough so that it will not become clogged with tea leaves.

1. The bowl of the teapot should be thrown with a thick enough lip to allow for an inner rim.

2. The lip and rim are finished with a soft leather.

3. Measurements for the lid must be accurate. Both parts should be thrown with clay of identical moisture content.

4

4. The lid is thrown upside down with a deep flange.
5. Immediately after trimming a knob is thrown on the lid.
6. The knob and lid may either harmonize with the vessel form or emerge as a contrasting element.
7. The base of the spout should be large enough to allow for considerable trimming.
8. The thrown handle is quite functional and relates well with the spout.

5

7

6

8

9. It is essential that the various parts of the teapot be of the same moisture content before they are joined.

10. The spout and handle are cut to fit the vessel. A thick slip is coated on both surfaces before joining.

11. The strainer holes should be large enough not to clog with glaze. The volume of the holes should be equal to or slightly larger than the spout opening.

12. After joining the teapot should be placed in a damp box for a day or two to allow any unevenness in the moisture content to equalize.

9

11

10

12

Stoneware teapot, similar to the one thrown on pages 36–38, with a wax-resist and stain decoration.

This stoneware coffee set with its full rounded forms has been finished with a rutile glaze. Robert Eckels.

The Upside-down Wheel

Sheldon Carey uses an unusual wheel for his special method of throwing. The beginner who is having trouble in raising even a 10-inch cylinder may be discouraged by this technique, but the photos should be of interest to those of a more inventive mind. This method is, of course, not necessarily an easy way to throw a cylinder, and is not meant for the novice. The walls must be perfectly uniform and decrease gradually in thickness. An air bubble or a thin spot will result in the clay being wrapped around the thrower's arm or lying in his lap.

1. The wheel is turned by a Denver electric motor mounted on an adjustable shaft.

2. After the clay has been centered and formed into a low cylinder, the wheel is reversed.

3. The throwing must be done cautiously. The technique is entirely different from that normally used; the clay is pulled down rather than built up.

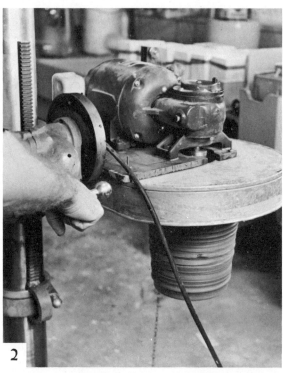

2

1

3

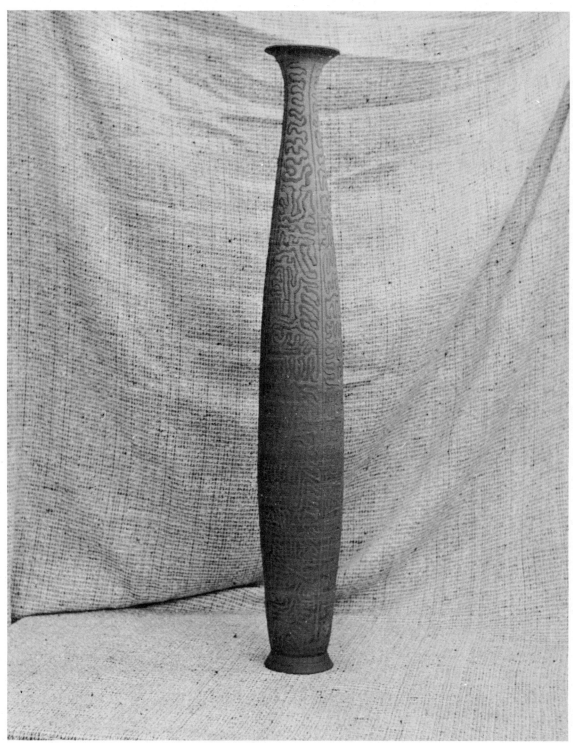

A 34-inch bottle thrown upside down. Sheldon Carey.

The Coiled Pot

Coiling is a pottery technique which goes back to the misty reaches of time. It requires no equipment other than the clay and is ideal both for teaching in the public school and the beginning pottery student. For the advanced potter it is foolish to coil forms which can be more easily made on the wheel. On the other hand, asymmetrical shapes, unless the potter distorts wheel pieces, can only be made by slab or coiling methods. Likewise, groggy clay, which can be thrown only with difficulty, is ideal for coiling.

1. A round pad is used as a base and a wad of clay is squeezed into a rope.

2. In rolling the coil, the entire hand from heel to finger tips is used. Rolling begins at the ends, and works towards the middle.

3. The coil circles the base pad and in three or four turns forms the wall of the pot.

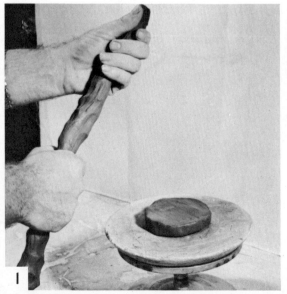

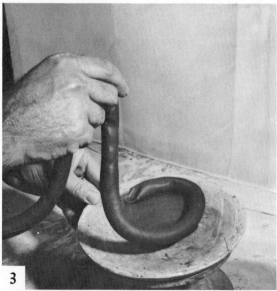

4. The coils are joined together inside and out, with an up-and-down wiping motion of the finger.
5. Another series of coils is added. The inside must be finished as work progresses.
6. Modeling tools as well as the fingers may be used to join the coils.
7. The outside form is refined with a flexible metal scraper.
8. The finished bottle has a textured decoration and hollow combination handle and filling mouth.

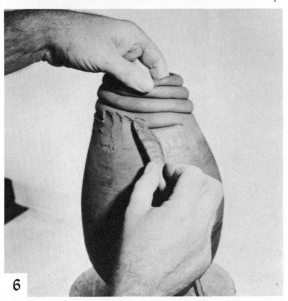

The Slab

Used alone or in combination with coiling the slab method allows one to make a variety of vertical forms or even flat trays without the use of either a wheel or mold. New shapes, quite unlike the original clay slab, may be made by cutting out sections and rejoining them. A simple method of forming is illustrated on the opposite page. Below are three interesting slab-constructed bottles by Angelo Garzio, U.S.A. The tops were thrown on the wheel and glazed with Albany slip. A mat white glaze is worked into the incised design. (Reduction fire at cone 10.)

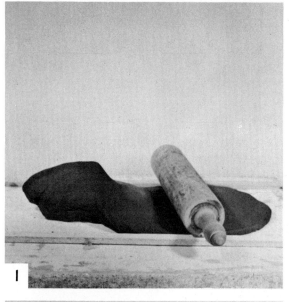

1. The clay slab is rolled to the desired thickness on a large plaster bat.

2. Top and bottom pieces are cut out.

3. Pinch marks left in joining form an effective decorative pattern.

4. Surfaces are coated with slip before joining.

5. An oval bottle is formed with the spout and feet added.

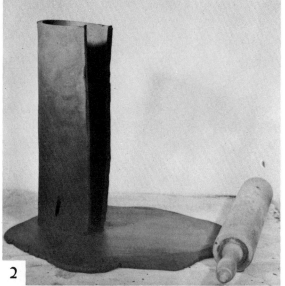

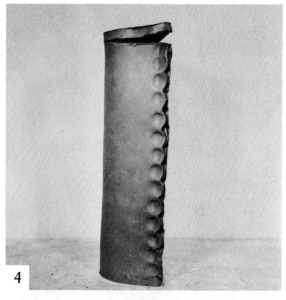

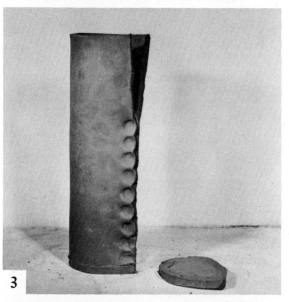

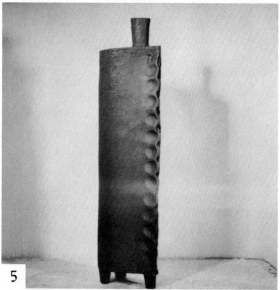

The Sand Mold

The use of the sand mold will eliminate the repetitive character which often occurs if plaster hump molds are used in the studio. The ease with which simple forms may be shaped with the wet sand will encourage more experimentation. A small amount of clay added to ordinary beach sand will enable the damp sand to hold its shape.

1. An oval shape is modeled in the wet sand.
2. Wet paper towels will keep the sand out of the clay.
3. The clay slab is placed over the sand mold, pressed into shape, and smoothed out.
4. Foot supports of various types may be added.
5. When it is leather hard, the rim is trimmed to its final form.

3

1

4

2

5

The thick wall of this groggy hand-built pot permits a deeply carved decoration. The design pattern is further emphasized by the contrast between the raw clay and glazed areas. Dirk Hubers.

The ceramic fountain offers an endless variety of
possibilities and is too seldom found in American
homes and gardens. This one is 26 inches high.
William Parry.

CHAPTER 4

CERAMIC SCULPTURE

The potential of ceramic sculpture in its many aspects has only recently
attracted the attention of today's ceramist. The time is most opportune
as the frozen cube of modern architecture is crying out for some manner
of adornment. The façades and lobbies of public and commercial buildings are generally barren and devoid of interest. This is an endeavor calling
for the combined efforts of both the architect and the ceramist. But this
will develop only if the potter is willing to experiment and to expand his
outlook.

On the following pages there are a number of recent works in the area of
ceramic sculpture. It is a varied group, but whether sculpture is in the
round, a fountain, or on decorative relief panels, each serves to make life
around it just a little more exciting. The facile nature of clay working
and the relative quickness of execution dictates for many a freedom of
expression in a more whimsical manner than is usual in other sculptural
media. The durable nature of stoneware and the wide range of textural,
color, and glaze effects would indicate a growing use of ceramic sculpture
in both the home and commercial buildings.

At the end of the chapter several methods used in forming ceramic sculpture are illustrated. While the pieces formed are rather traditional and
not too complicated in form, the general techniques are the same since
the clay must be joined, dried, and fired under roughly the same conditions regardless of the size or style.

(Top) "Little Big Horn," a 5½-foot-high ceramic sculpture, is constructed of thrown stoneware and slab shapes. Peter Voulkos. London Gallery, Los Angeles.

(Opposite, top) These stoneware mural panels are done in high relief. 7 x 9 feet. John Mason. Abbott residence, Los Angeles.

(Opposite, bottom) The interest in this low-relief mural is centered in the textural design and slip decoration. Cone 5 with iron and copper washes, 6 x 6 feet. Henry Takemoto.

The Ceramic Mural

One of the most successful projects in recent decorative wall treatments is the ceramic mural designed and executed by Frans Wildenhain for the Strasenburgh Laboratories in Rochester, New York. The over-all view below gives some idea of the wall size (12 x 100 feet) as well as the suitability of the ceramic design to the architectural concept and furnishings of this unique lounge and lobby.

On the opposite page are successive closeups illustrating one of the ceramic units: flower and nature forms showing the sources of medicines. The silhouette shapes and textural effects are very exciting. The mural is particularly notable for the richness of its slip, stain, and glaze combinations.

Photo by Minor White

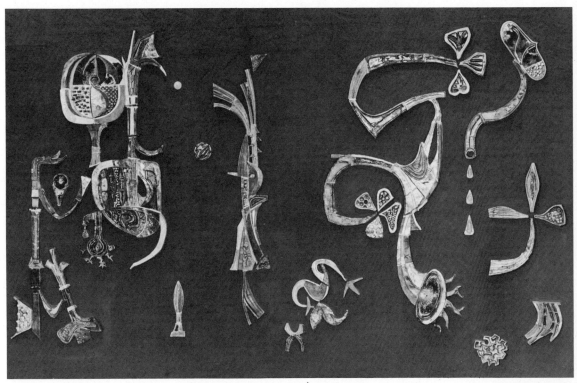

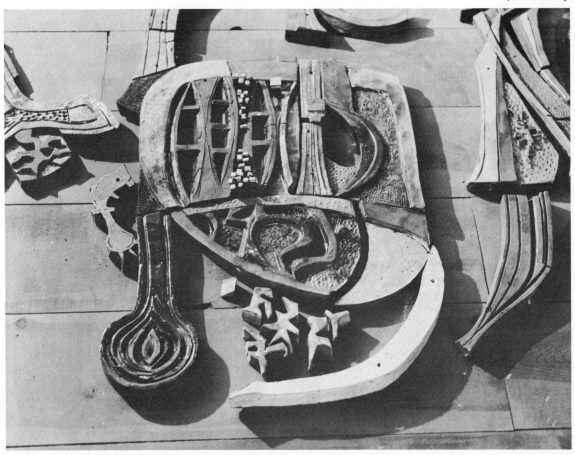

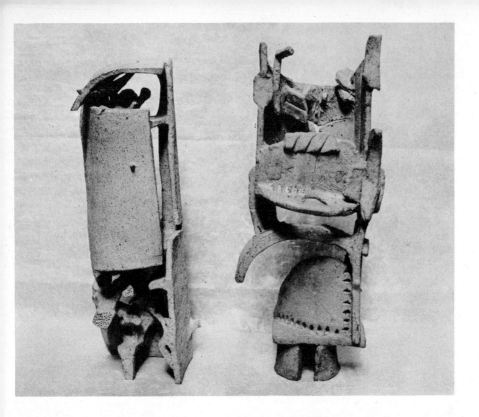

(Above) Detail, "Lady of Sorrows." Terra cotta, 33 inches high. Kenneth M. Green.

(Left, above). Two sculptural forms. Stoneware reduction with manganese body flecks, cone 8-10, 28 inches high. Ted Beilefeld.

(Left, below) Interlocking clay structures. Stoneware, 6 feet high. John Mason. Ferus Gallery.

The Solid Form

MODELING A PORTRAIT HEAD

Of all the methods of forming ceramic sculpture, the solid form, which is later hollowed out, is the easiest. Of course, sculpture can be made in a mold, but the pieces thus formed are like molded pots because they lack surface color and texture. By comparison with the original, the mold-made piece tends to lack definition of form. To facilitate drying and to reduce shrinkage the sculpture clay should contain about 20-percent grog (crushed insulation bricks, flower pots, and so forth).

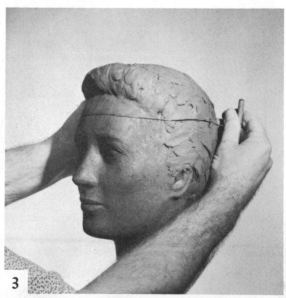

1. A coffee can forms a simple armature. Butterflies—wood blocks on wire—prevent the clay from slipping down the pipe.

2. The completed head is covered with a plastic bag between poses to prevent drying out.

3. The top of the head is cut off with a double twisted copper wire.

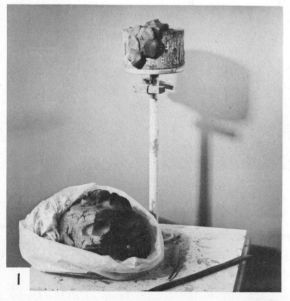

4. The top section and the head proper are hollowed out, leaving a wall thickness of approximately ¾ of an inch.

5. After both surfaces have been coated with slip, the two sections are joined.

6. After firing the neck section is filled with plaster or cement to support a large lag screw.

7. The finished portrait is slightly waxed and mounted on a mahogany block.

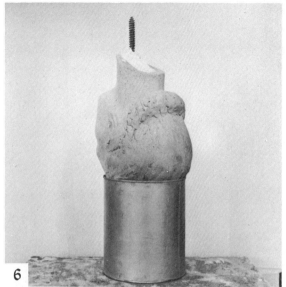

6

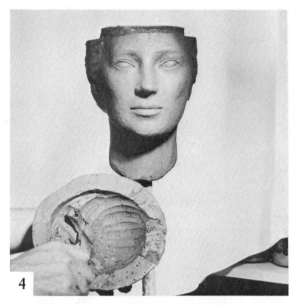

4

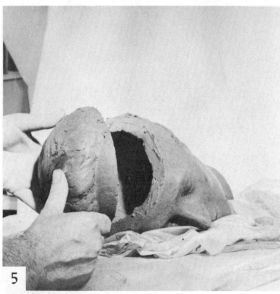

5

7

FLAT-COIL CONSTRUCTION

Flat-coil construction is a relatively rapid method of building up a simple ceramic form. Since the ceramist must start from the bottom and work up and only minor alterations can be made during the process, a fairly accurate sketch should be prepared beforehand. The walls should be kept to between ¾ to 1 inch in thickness. A center partition can be built in for support.

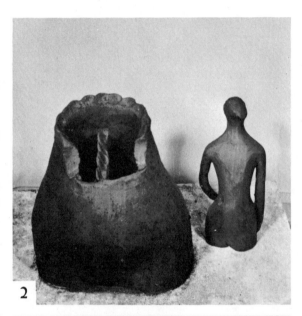

1. A 2-inch coil of clay is flattened to form the slab sections.

2. By beveling the clay edge the slabs are easily joined.

3. A dowel is used to form the arms which are hollowed to facilitate·drying and thus lessen the possibility of cracking.

This head study was built up hollow with a center partition. The grog was composed of crushed insulating brick and soft red building bricks. Very thin glazes were used to bring out the clay and grog color.

4. A nail holds the arm in place. After the arm has dried slightly, the clay is added to develop the form.

5. Before drying starts, the arms are wrapped with damp paper towels. Do not hurry the final drying period.

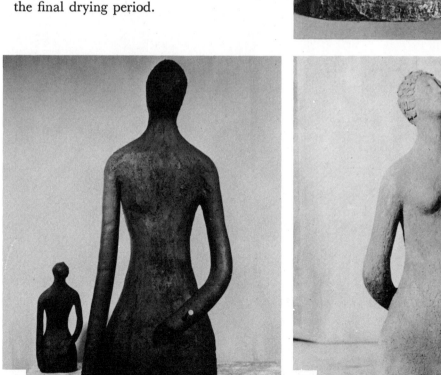

4

5

TUBE CONSTRUCTIONS

The troublesome aspect of ceramic sculpture is the drying stage. The piece must dry slowly and uniformly so that it will not develop cracks which will only become enlarged upon firing. The tube method, illustrated here in several sequence photos, largely avoids this problem. An air passage running through the arms and legs into the hollow torso is constructed.

1. Clay tubes are formed over a dowel or section of a pipe.

2. The leg tubes enlarge into the torso and at first need several supports.

3. The torso is built up by the flat-coil method. Clay is added gradually to build up the forms.

This ceramic figure, about 2½ feet high, was constructed by the tube method. No difficulty was encountered in drying or firing.

4. A hollow clay support is needed to hold the figure up. It will later serve as a kiln support.

5. The groggy surface is one of the attractions of ceramic sculpture. The final modeling should not obscure it.

4

5

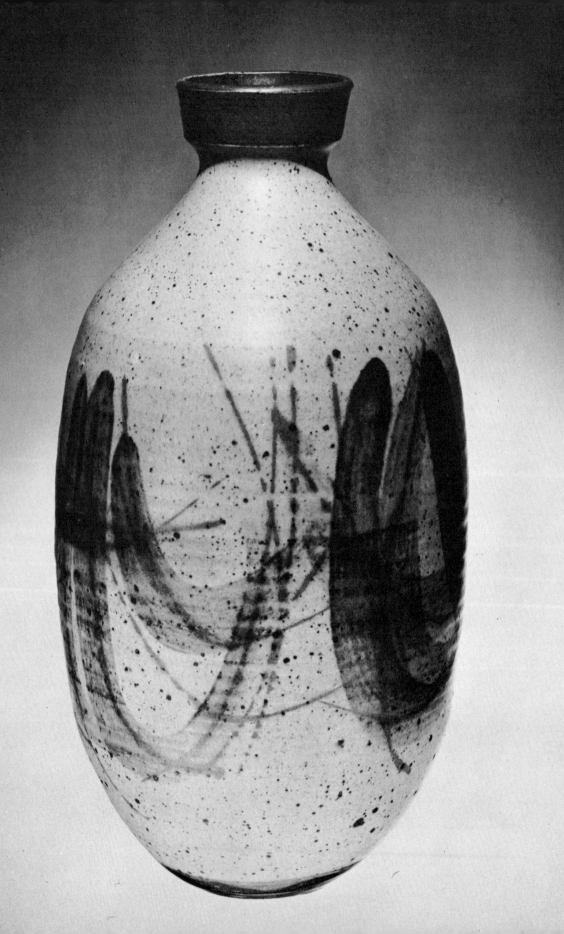

A simple shape can become rather dramatic. The freely brushed linear decoration is accented by the vase's strong rim. Albany and copper-bearing slips were used under a Cornwall glaze. Harvey Littleton.

CHAPTER 5

CERAMIC DECORATION

Whenever decoration is suggested, the question always comes up, "If the shape is good, isn't a simple glaze enough?" The answer is yes. The only trouble is that in time one becomes tired of perfect shapes with perfect glazes and yearns for a little variety—in short, some decoration. Decoration is a process which most beginning potters back into hesitatingly. It should not be so. Rather, the approach should be one of experimentation. After all, there is nothing final about decoration. There are few designs which cannot be easily altered.

The important point to remember is that decoration exists to enhance the form of a particular pot, to make it more attractive and pleasing to the eye. Bas-relief sculpture, painted pictures, or smeary designs do little to enhance the form of an object. Clay and clay vessels have a certain quality which, by itself, makes some types of decorations more suitable than others.

Perhaps equally important are the cultural factors which influence the desirability of certain shapes and decorations. It is very difficult for students to realize that repeating the shape and design motifs of the past, however excellent they may be, is not sufficient for the potter today. A portrait-head Mochica stirrup pot or a Persian Rakka bowl are beautiful possessions to own and to see in a collection. To imitate them, however, is a mistake. It is impossible to recapture the spirit of a past age with conviction. We should not, on the other hand, snobbishly ignore the past, refuse to enjoy its products, or fail to profit from its technical and esthetic achievements.

Photo by Louis Reens

The Museum of Contemporary Crafts in New York City has continuous exhibits of crafts in a setting which is, in itself, a striking example of fine design.

We ought to take advantage of every opportunity to visit museums, particularly contemporary craft exhibitions. Of special interest is the new Museum of Contemporary Crafts in New York City. In addition to its continually changing exhibits, it has a craft library and a slide collection. America House, which serves as the sales and display center for many Eastern craftsmen, is also a worthwhile stop in New York.

Although there is little in America to compare with the numerous design exhibitions in Europe, the situation is improving. Much more could be accomplished if school and community galleries were more enterprising. There are many fine craft exhibits available for only the shipping and insurance charges. A few fine collections in various media are circulated by the American Craftsmen's Council. Of special interest to potters is the biannual traveling show selected by the Ceramic National Exhibition in Syracuse, New York. Various regional organizations, such as the Mid-West Designer-Craftsmen and the St. Paul Gallery, also make up attractive traveling exhibits from their annual shows. Information on additional exhibitions may be found in *Craft Horizons* and other magazines in the craft field.

Exhibitions are important not only to the student but to the public at large. Much of the so-called poor public taste may be blamed, in part, to the lack of opportunity to see good work. *Den Permanente*, a nonprofit organization in Copenhagen which operates a most attractive store, has

A display of Saxbo stoneware in the famous crafts-men's store, *Den Permanente*, Copenhagen, Denmark. Only through such an organization can a small pottery enjoy a downtown outlet.

This handsome staircase in *Den Permanente* is an ex-ample of the care and importance given to the display of crafts abroad; it leads to the second floor where glass and silverware are displayed.

had an important influence upon other shops all over Denmark. About 350 Danish craftsmen and manufacturers exhibit and sell their products here. Because it handles only well-designed pieces, it has encouraged many other stores to upgrade their merchandise.

Nearby Sweden has a slightly different approach. In a park adjoining Stockholm's main shopping center there are about a dozen large glass display cases installed by the Swedish Industrial Design Society, which selects items of especially good design from retail stores in the neighbor-hood for display. Because of their location in the park with an outdoor restaurant and bubbling fountains nearby, the displays are an outstanding attraction.

Whether anything similar is feasible in the United States I do not know. It might be argued that teachers have a responsibility beyond merely teaching techniques and advocating art principles. Art must be brought into the community and become a part of daily living. The crafts generally and ceramics in particular have an advantage in this respect, combining

Finnish ceramics and glass displayed in a Scandinavian good-design trade fair in Sweden. The display, itself, epitomizes fine design.

An outdoor showcase in downtown Stockholm's Kungstradgardsgatan's Park, displaying well-designed merchandise available in nearby shops.

as they do functional use with esthetic value. There is a definite need for the individual touch in an increasingly stereotyped society such as ours. The mass production of the machine does not satisfy these dimly felt but real psychological needs. How to serve this function is the problem of design. The techniques of ceramics are secondary to their design. The term design encompasses the form and the decoration as well as the function of a piece.

What should be the direction of contemporary ceramics? This is a difficult question. It cannot be answered by looking backward toward the past. Contemporary art in any form is related to the society and culture which produces it. There is a very definite relationship between ceramics and contemporary architecture, painting, sculpture, industrial design, and interior decoration. Perhaps by comparing contemporary design and the design of the preceding Victorian Era we can identify those features which are significantly different to be classed as characteristic of our age. Contemporary design is influenced by the Bauhaus concept of functionalism. Under the influence of this philosophy, most manufacturers have eliminated the cast-iron roses and stenciled flowers which were once felt to be the necessary decoration of mass-produced goods. The frank and honest use of material is a characteristic of the better-designed products today. For example, today's manufacturer no longer feels it necessary to disguise metal with an imitation wood grain. Gradually, however, the Bauhaus concept has been modified: machine-made functionalism does not satisfy both our esthetic and material wants. Man, performing for the most part monotonous repetitive tasks during the day, unconsciously rebels at returning to a home furnished with mass-produced objects identical to those of his neighbors. The arts in any age respond to the economic and cultural needs of the particular period. What they may happen to be at the moment is something dimly, and perhaps subconsciously, felt.

Today two schools of thought influence the trend of contemporary ceramics. One group feels that the potter should produce handmade pots of a more or less functional nature at a price which the average person can afford. This is the concept of the traditional craftsman potter. The other faction would leave the functional to the factory and proposes that ceramists make only decorative pieces. But decoration, in itself, implies a function. On the other hand, many extremely functional pieces can be esthetically satisfying in their over-all design. Each viewpoint has a certain merit. My only quarrel is with those who insist on limiting themselves to making pot sculptures. Clay, and sculpture itself, has no implied form. It is free. While an occasional sculpturelike form may evolve on the wheel, in practice the wheel is a limitation under which a sculptor can work only to his eventual creative disadvantage.

It is most difficult to evaluate a new form or concept in art. The immature person tends to react negatively to new ideas or situations. In the arts we are gradually trained to look upon the new and different with favor since "new" connotes that dreadful but desirable word, "creativity."

More than ever before art forms today seem to emphasize the new and different, perhaps reflecting in many ways the rapidity of change so characteristic of the commercial world. Contemporary art exhibitions set great store in being avant-garde, and interpretive catalogue introductions with their bewildering jargon hardly assist the observer. Of course, lacking the perspective of time, it is impossible to judge contemporary artistic expression. In order to develop truly creative expression, the student must first learn his craft thoroughly, keeping an open mind toward all work in his field, historical or contemporary. The most important ingredient is plain hard work. The specialized approach must be avoided.

It must be remembered that creamics is not alien to painting or sculpture. All the various art forms, verbal and aural as well as visual and plastic, are interrelated. The expression of the artist is not produced in a vacuum. It must be an adequate esthetic reflection of the total social environment.

The creation of such an expression requires more than a planned course of studies. The ways of art, like life itself, are, if not accidental, at least mysterious and to an extent beyond evident human control.

In the balance of this section, no attempt will be made to develop a design concept. This is basically a problem which can be solved only in the studio by interaction between the student, the material, and the teacher. Instead, a brief summary and a few illustrations of the various methods of decoration will follow. We hope it will serve to indicate to the beginner some of the possibilities of decoration and will function, as well, as a useful guide for the student who may later wish to teach ceramics.

Clay Prior to Forming

Clay can be treated in several ways to enhance its future decorative possibilities. In many cases the effectiveness of textural and glaze effects depends upon the preliminary treatment of the clay body.

Clays can be blended in various proportions. Such combinations increase the variety of body color and texture.

Coloring oxides may be added. As a rule it is better to mix the coloring oxides in water first and then add them to the clay in a slip form. Red iron oxide and manganese dioxide are the two most common coloring oxides used, since many of the others, like cobalt and vanadium, are much too expensive to use in a body but are used instead in a slip form of decorating. When adding manganese, be sure that the amount does not exceed 7 percent; otherwise the clay will blister when fired.

Grog can be added for texture. Grog is usually made of fire clay or a similar type of clay which is fired and then ground and sifted to various particle sizes. Grog can be made easily by crushing soft insulating brick. Most commercial grogs on the market are light grey or white. For a dark grog first bisque fire some dark clay, and then pound and sift it. Old bricks of the soft red variety make good grog because they break up easily. Since these bricks were not fired at very high temperatures, grog made from them will fire a dark brown at cone 04. Grog can also be made of a coarse flint sand bearing various metallic impurities, such as the black iron sand from the Lake Superior region. Before adding a coarse sand grog test it for particles of limestone. Limestone and plaster particles dehydrate in the kiln. Later in the room atmosphere, they absorb moisture, expand,

Several stoneware bottles displaying a variety of impressed designs. Sheldon Carey.

and small sections pop out of the body, leaving pits in the vessel. In extreme cases the whole piece will disintegrate. Limestone in the grog is not troublesome if the piece is fired to cone 8 or above in a single fire glaze (no bisque firing). At these higher temperatures the limestone or plaster melts and becomes part of the body. As it is so easy to make a mistake, it is best not to use lime-bearing sand as grog.

Clay in the Plastic State

In the plastic state clay has a limited number of decorative possibilities, the chief of which are discussed here.

Natural ornamentation can be caused by the fingers either in throwing on the wheel or by shaping hand-built pieces. The concentric spirals in a bowl and the ridges left on a bottle by the pressure of the fingers are the simplest and often most effective decoration since they express the unique quality of clay—its plasticity. Glazes later applied will tend to collect in these depressions, further enhancing the effect.

Impressed designs are best applied while the clay is in this soft state. Simple negative dies may be cut from rubber erasers or modeled in clay and bisque fired. They can be made in a circular form with a center hole and can be fitted with a pin and a roller handle. Other materials, such as a coarse twisted cord, may be used to impart texture. The impressed design was perhaps the earliest form of decoration used by primitive man, but it can be just as effective today.

Covered jar thrown as a sphere. The lid has been cut off and a coiled rim added. The wax-resist decoration under the glaze is very effective. Tom Sellers.

Stoneware bowl with an extremely interesting pressed decoration. Theodore Randall.

Leather-hard Clay

Leather-hard clay is generally preferred for most decorative processes. At this stage the shape of the pot is fully realized and the final decoration can be planned more completely. The vessel, although still damp, is hard enough to be handled conveniently and without injury.

Tooling and burnishing done while the vessel is on the wheel can add a variety of textures. Wire, wood, and metal tools of various types can be used. Old dental tools are excellent for trimming and incising purposes. Bone tools are better for burnishing.

Carving. Relief ornamentation can be made by cutting with a sharp tool or fine wire loop. These tools are best adapted for carved types of decoration.

Incising. For a lineal decoration, designs can be cut into the clay with a sharp tool.

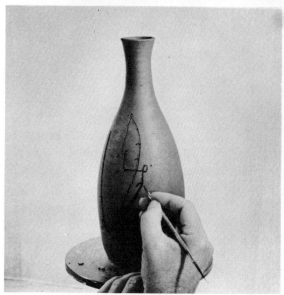

Inlay or "Mishima" is a continuation of the incising process. After the incisions have been cut into the clay, they are filled with a thick slip of a contrasting colored clay. When the clay is partially dried, the excess slip is scraped off flush with the surface.

Slip painting is another old and common type of decoration. Contrasting colored slips may be either poured, brushed, or sprayed onto the clay body. The piece should not be too dry. If additional moisture has to be applied on one side or in a limited area, it may cause the clay to expand unevenly and crack. The slip may also peel off upon drying if the body is too dry. The slip design may be limited to skillful calligraphic brushwork in an oriental fashion. Skillful brushwork will require a little practice. Use a Chinese watercolor brush; its stiffness is better suited for working with slip.

Sgraffito designs are made by scratching or scraping through a layer of applied slip to expose the contrasting color of the clay body beneath.

Slip trailing is a method by which slip is trailed over a piece from a syringe in much the same manner as decorating a cake. The body must not be too dry or the slip will fall off when it dries.

Sprigging is the application of press-molded clay ornaments to the surface of the vessel by means of a clay slip. This is the same method by which handles and spouts are joined to a pot. It is important that both pieces have the same moisture content; otherwise the joined pieces will crack off upon drying.

Pâte sur pâte refers to a relief design built up by coating parts of the body with successive layers of slip.

Clay in the Dry State

Several of the processes such as sprigging, carving, incising, and sgraffito can also be performed when clay is in the dry state. They are, however, more difficult to perform when the clay is dry, and it is usually impossible to repair damage in case mishaps occur.

Wax-resist decoration can be effectively combined with colored stains when clay is in the dry state. Beeswax, thinned with turps and heated, may be used although commercial water-soluble wax emulsions are more convenient.

Coloring oxides or stains are best applied when the clay is dry. The bisque fire will cause the decoration to adhere so that the ware can be handled without damage during the glazing operation. While the ware need not be bone dry, it must be sufficiently absorbent so that the stain will not run. If a very watery stain is used on thin, dry ware, cracking may result. If an excessive amount of colorant is used, the overglaze may not adhere well. For example, too much manganese will cause the glaze to blister.

A *sgraffito* design scratched through a wax area allows a sharper linear pattern than does any other means. The illustrations on this page show the application of the wax and an incised sgraffito design. The stain covers all areas of the dry clay not coated with wax. In the bisque fire the wax burns off completely.

Clay in the Bisque State

Glazes are generally applied when the clay body is in a bisque state. In addition to glazing, there are other ways of decorating clay in this state.

An engobe decoration or an over-all coat of slip may be applied provided the slip has somewhat the character of a glaze. In other words, the clay must naturally contain some fluxes (like Albany slip), or fluxes, feldspar, and silica must be added in order for the slip to unite with the body upon firing. The contraction rate of the slip must be small or it will peel off upon drying or upon firing. (See "Slip Glazes.")

An underglaze of coloring oxides, colored stains, or underglaze colors may also be applied. The coloring oxides have a greater tendency to run into the glaze than the relatively insoluble spinel-type colored stains. The glaze may be poured or sprayed directly over the stain decoration, although this is not the usual method of applying an underglaze decoration. Underglaze colors consist of a colored spinel stain, a flux, and a diluent like silica or alumina to control shrinkage and the firing temperature.

Both color stains and underglaze colors are usually mixed with either oil and turpentine, gum and water, or glycerine and water when they are applied to biscuit ware. The ware must then undergo an extra firing to a red heat which will burn out the adhesives before the glaze is applied. Failure to do so will generally result in bubbles or blisters over the decorated areas. Commercially, an underglaze decoration is used where an overglaze might wear off, such as for the stripes on restaurant china. Due to the relatively insoluble character of color-stain spinels sharp effects are possible. Decorations which have a softer quality can be easily made by mixing coloring oxides with a small amount of the overglaze. (See the section on coloring oxides, stains, and underglaze colors.)

Inlaid colors. Incised decorations can be filled with either colored glazes or stains. After the surface has been wiped clean, the vessel can be sprayed with either a transparent or semitransparent glaze.

Pottery is usually glazed in the bisque state because bisque ware can be handled with greater safety and ease than raw ware. Glazes may be either poured, dipped, brushed, or sprayed, depending upon the shape of the vessel and the facilities available. (See Chapter 6, pp. 77-80.) Decorations in underglaze color may also be painted on a vessel previously coated with an opaque glaze, preferably one that has been poured. This is the technique used to produce majolica ware.

Wax-resist decoration is painted· on the bisque with a solution of heated wax. When the glaze is later applied, it will run off the portions coated with wax. The effect of the contrast between the body and the glaze must be considered since the decoration will appear in the clay body color upon firing.

The wax need not be applied to the bisque, but may instead be brushed onto a layer of glaze with a second coating of glaze then sprayed on top. This will produce quite a different effect than the clay-body and glaze contrast discussed above. Although it is not as easily controlled, the use of rubber cement has certain advantages. Since it may be peeled off after glazing, the definition is sharper, whereas the glaze often piles up at the edges of a wax design.

Sgraffito designs may also be scratched through the glaze coating to expose either the clay body or a preliminary glaze. In order for the scratched design to be sharp and clean, the glaze must be slightly damp and not too thick or it will chip, leaving a ragged edge.

For every form there is one type of glaze or decoration that is more suitable than others. Each of these stoneware vases has been glazed differently. Marguerite Wildenhain.

CHAPTER 6

GLAZING AND GLAZE DEFECTS

While there is no substitute for actual experience in glazing, it may be helpful to list a few of the recommended procedures to supplement and perhaps make clearer classroom demonstrations. For the student who may want to teach ceramics or work in it after a lapse of several years, the following brief summary may prove useful as a future reference.

When to Glaze

When to glaze depends upon several factors. For the studio potter, the type of decoration employed will have a considerable effect upon the time when the piece should be glazed. In commercial production, economies of labor and fuel are the deciding factors.

Glazing in the raw-clay state has been mentioned briefly in the section on decoration. There are definite advantages to this method. By eliminating the normal bisque fire, there are savings not only in the labor involved in the extra stacking, unloading, and operation of the kiln, but in the fuel or power needed for the extra firing. A single firing also promotes a better union between the body and the glaze. There are several disadvantages, however, to the single glaze fire, chief of which is the fragile nature of the raw, dry clay vessel. Not only is it apt to be broken in handling but the expansions caused by the moisture absorbed into the dry clay may cause the vessel to crack. In general, only when the body of a piece is rather thick and uniform can the glaze be poured safely. Other pieces should be sprayed since the glaze, with its troublesome moisture content, can then be applied at a slower rate. One additional precaution must be observed in glazing raw ware. As mentioned before, alkaline fluxes must first be fritted before they can be safely used on raw ware. These compounds have a high coefficient of thermal expansion. When they are absorbed into the outer portion of the clay, their expansion and contraction rate during firing and cooling is so great in contrast to the remainder of the body that they will cause it to crack. Much the same thing will happen in a normal glaze firing if the glaze and the body have greatly different expansion rates.

Glazing in the bisque state is the most common procedure. Normally the bisque ware is fired to about cone 010 (1650° F). At this stage the bisque is hard enough to be handled safely, yet porous enough to absorb the glaze readily. A bisque fired either too high or too low is especially difficult to glaze since it tends to absorb too much glaze or the glaze tends to run off. An exception to the normal bisque firings are the high-fired chinawares. Such pieces, like thin teacups, which are fragile and tend to warp, are often placed in the kiln with supporting fire-clay rings inside their lips, or they are stacked upside down and then fired to their maximum temperature. Later these chinaware pieces are glazed and fired on their own foot rims at a lower temperature where warpage losses are much less.

Overglazing is generally a decorative procedure, although occasionally it may be used to remedy an initial glaze which was applied too thinly or to cover a displeasing color effect or decoration. (See the section on overglaze decoration.)

How to Glaze

Glazing is a process which can be described only rather inadequately. Before the actual glazing operation takes place, however, there are a few precautions which must be observed. If the bisque ware is not to be glazed immediately upon its removal from the glaze kiln, it should be stored, if possible, where dust and soot will not settle on it. The bisque ware should not be handled excessively especially if the hands are oily with perspiration. Perspiration will prevent the glaze from adhering properly.

All surfaces of the bisque ware should be wiped with a damp sponge or momentarily placed under a water tap to remove dust and loose particles of clay. The moisture added to the bisque ware will prevent an excessive amount of glaze from soaking in and thus allow a little more time for glazing.

It also helps to reduce the number of air pockets and pinholes which form when the glaze dries too quickly on a very porous bisque. The amount of moisture required depends upon the absorbency of the bisque, the thickness of the piece, and the consistency of the glaze. Should the bisque fire accidentally rise much higher than cone 010, the ware should not be dampened at all. As is so often the case in pottery making, there is no sure rule for obtaining the perfect effect. Good results are achieved only by experience, by thinking out every problem, and by learning from mistakes.

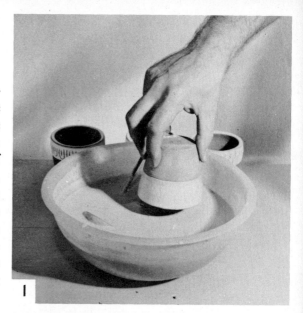

Dip glazing is perhaps the simplest glazing method. Its chief drawback is that a rather large amount of glaze is required. After the vessel has been cleaned and moistened with a damp sponge, it is plunged into a large pan of glaze. It should be withdrawn almost immediately and shaken to remove the excess glaze. The object is then placed upon a rack to dry and the finger marks are touched up with a brush. Commercial producers handle the pieces with metal tongs which leave smaller blemishes to be repaired. When dry, the glaze is cleaned off completely from the bottom and foot rim and about 1/8 of an inch up the sides.

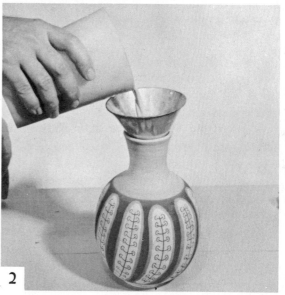

Poured glazes require less initial glaze than dip glazes and can be applied to a greater variety of shapes. For example, the insides of bottles and deep vaselike vessels can be glazed only in this manner. In the case of a bottle, the glaze is poured through a funnel and then the vessel is rotated until all its surfaces are covered. Then the excess is poured out and the bottle is given a final shake to even out the glaze and remove the excess. Glazes which are poured or dipped have to be a little thinner in consistency than those which are brushed on. The interior of bowls may be glazed by pouring in a portion of the glaze, rolling the

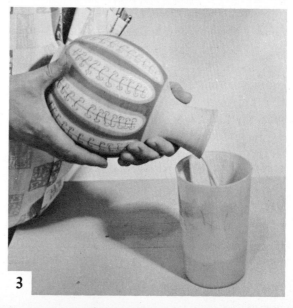

(1) For a dip-glaze effect, the decorative band of the cup is quickly dipped into a transparent glaze. (2) To glaze the inside of a bottle, pour a quantity of glaze into it; (3) then rapidly rotate the bottle quickly so that the glaze will pour out slowly.

bowl around, and then pouring out the excess. Generally this must be done rather quickly or an excessive or an uneven amount of glaze will accumulate. To glaze the exterior of bottles, grasp them by either the neck or the foot rim and pour the glaze over the bottle from a pitcher, allowing the excess to run off into a pan beneath. Finger marks are then touched up with a brush and the foot cleaned when it is dry. The exterior of bowls may be glazed in the same manner provided the foot is large enough to grasp; otherwise the bowl may be placed upside down on wooden dowel rods extending across a pan. It is the best practice to glaze the interior of vessels first and the outside later.

Brushed glazes are generally used to apply a band or decorative panel of glaze. Small pieces may be glazed satisfactorily by brush, but in glazing large pieces, it is difficult to obtain an even coating. In some cases, an elephant-ear sponge may be used in place of the brush. With practice, a large area can be evenly covered. Brush glazes are usually used in children's classes since the pieces are generally small and the youngsters will waste less glaze with this method than by pouring or dipping. Low-temperature and runny glazes are best suited to the brushing method.

Sprayed glazes permit subtle variations in color and more definite control over glaze thickness and coverage. Actually these advantages are more theoretical than real and apply more to the beginner than the experienced potter. The finest Chinese glazes of the past, which we have difficulty in equaling today, were all dipped or poured. Gradations of color were achieved by blowing the color on separately through a lung-powered, bamboo tube atomizer.

(1) To pour glaze over the under side of a bowl, mount the bowl on a pan or another bowl to catch the overflow. (2) A brushed glaze must be applied quickly with a 1-inch flat brush, using overlapping strokes. (3) To build up a uniform coat, apply sprayed glazes evenly.

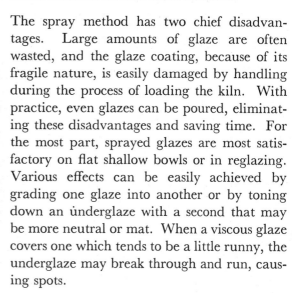

The spray method has two chief disadvantages. Large amounts of glaze are often wasted, and the glaze coating, because of its fragile nature, is easily damaged by handling during the process of loading the kiln. With practice, even glazes can be poured, eliminating these disadvantages and saving time. For the most part, sprayed glazes are most satisfactory on flat shallow bowls or in reglazing. Various effects can be easily achieved by grading one glaze into another or by toning down an underglaze with a second that may be more neutral or mat. When a viscous glaze covers one which tends to be a little runny, the underglaze may break through and run, causing spots.

As many glaze materials are toxic, glazes should be sprayed only in a booth with an adequate exhaust fan. In order to obtain an even layer of glaze, one should spray the glaze on slowly, building up a coating with a soft "woolly" surface. If the sprayed piece gets too moist, a wet shine may develop, blisters may form, and the glaze may run. If the glaze runs, it will be uneven, regardless of how much more glaze is used. It may be advisable, then, under some conditions to scrape off the glaze and start again. When the bottoms of bowls are being glazed, the foot rims should be protected. Various-sized jar lids may be placed over the rims, thereby avoiding the later task of dry footing them, or a coating of wax can be used to prevent the glaze from adhering to the rim.

(1) If the glaze is too wet, it will run and cause blisters in the glaze. (2) Proper spraying leaves a "woolly" coating. The curved bottom portions should be sprayed slightly before the body is placed on the spinner.

Glaze Defects

All too often a well-thrown piece is spoiled by the imperfection of the glaze. This is especially true of student work. Glazing cannot be approached in a hit-or-miss fashion. With care and judgment glaze faults can be avoided.

If a mishap occurs, the student should immediately try to analyze his error so that he will not repeat it.

Usually there are several reasons, all logical, why a particular glaze fault may occur. Trying to deduce the cause from one piece may prove quite difficult. When there are available a number of pots having the same glaze from a single kiln load, or when there are several glazes on a single body, the problem of deduction is much easier. The section following outlines several factors which cause glaze defects. Glaze faults may result not only from the composition of the glaze but from the improper selection or preparation of the clay body, faulty kiln operation, or, as most frequently is the case, lack of skill and care in application.

DEFECTS DUE TO THE BODY

1. A body which to too porous because of improper wedging, kneading, blunging, or pugging may cause small bubbles, beads, and pinholes to form in the glaze as the body contracts and the gases attempt to escape.
2. Excessive water used in forming the piece may result in conditions somewhat similar to those above.
3. An excessive amount of manganese dioxide used as a colorant in a body or slip will cause blisters to form in both the body and the glaze.
4. Soluble sulfates are contained in some clays and come to the surface in drying, forming a whitish scum. Pinholes and bubbles are formed as these sulfates react with the glaze to form gases. This condition may be eliminated by adding 2 percent barium carbonate to the body. A slight reduction fire at the point at which the glaze begins to melt will reduce the sulfates and allow the gas to pass off before the glaze develops a glassy retaining film.
5. If the body is underfired in the bisque and therefore very porous, it may absorb an excessive amount of the glaze. Soluble fluxes in the glaze, because of their higher thermal expansion and contraction rates, may cause the body to crack. In any case a glaze applied to a very absorptive body may have a coarse if not sandpaperlike surface.

DEFECTS OF APPLICATION

1. Blisters or pinholes may result if the bisque has not been moistened slightly before glazing. The glaze traps air in the surface pores of the body.

2. Dust or oil on the surface of the bisque may cause pinholes or a scaley surface in the glaze.

3. If the glaze is applied too heavily, it will run excessively, obscuring the decoration and perhaps making the pot stick to the kiln shelves.

4. In addition to flowing excessively, glazes which have been applied too thickly will usually crack upon drying. As a rule, when they are fired, these cracks will not heal up but will pull further apart and bead up at the edges. If the drying contraction is great enough, the adhesion of the glaze to the body will be weak, causing portions to flake off during the initial smoking period of the firing cycle.

5. On the other hand, too thin a glaze application will result in a poor, dry surface. This is especially true of mat glazes, which, as a rule, require a slightly thicker application than gloss glazes.

6. If a second glaze coating is applied over a completely dry first coat, blisters will form. The wetting of the lower glaze layer causes it to expand and pull away from the body.

7. If the bisque ware is considerably cooler than the glaze at the time of application, bubbles and blisters may later develop.

DEFECTS ORIGINATING IN FIRING

1. If freshly glazed ware is placed in the kiln and fired immediately, the hot moisture will loosen the glaze from the body causing blisters and crawling.

2. Too rapid firing will not allow the normal gases to escape. They will form tiny seeds and bubbles in the glaze.

3. For some especially viscous glazes a prolonged soaking period is necessary to remove these gas bubbles.

4. Excessive reduction will result in black and gray spots on the body and glaze and a dull surface.

5. Gas-fired kilns with poor muffles using manufactured gas are troublesome to use with lead glazes. The sulphur content in the combustion gases will dull the glaze surfaces and possibly form blisters and wrinkles.

DEFECTS IN GLAZE COMPOSITION

1. Glazes which are not adjusted properly to the body are susceptible to stresses which may cause the glaze and at times even the body to crack. If the glaze contracts at a slower rate than the body does in cooling, it goes into *compression*, causing the glaze to crack and in

The interesting glaze effect on this covered stoneware jar and bottle is achieved by a colored grog which reacts with the glaze. Abe Cohn.

places to buckle up and separate from the body. This defect is more commonly known as *shivering*.

2. Slightly similar to shivering and also caused by unequal contraction rates in cooling is *crazing* of the glaze. In this case the glaze contracts at a greater rate than the body, causing numerous cracks to form. One common remedy is to add flint to either the body or the glaze. It seems strange that in either case the effect is approximately the same. This is due to the fact that flint (SiO_2) in a glaze converts to a crystalline state. In this form the silica undergoes only a limited thermal expansion, thus reducing the contraction of the glaze. When added to a clay body the silica combines with the fluxes to produce a denser body and one which necessarily contracts more in firing.

3. Glazes which run excessively during the normal firing temperatures should be adjusted by adding kaolin to increase the refractory quality of the glaze or, if possible, by changing the bases. Those which have a lower molecular weight will be less fluid in the glaze melt.

4. A dull surface will result if the proportion of silica to alumina or barium is too low.

5. An excessive amount of tin, rutile, or colored spinels which are rela-

tively insoluble in the glaze will also cause a dull or rough-surfaced glaze.

6. Bristol and colemanite glazes not fitted properly to the body will tend to crawl excessively or crack. This may be due in part to an excess of zinc which has a very high contraction rate at the upper temperatures.

7. Glazes ground too finely, thus releasing soluble salts from the frits, feldspars, and so forth, will develop pinholes and bubbles.

8. Glazes, if allowed to stand too long, may be affected by the decomposition of carbonates, organic matter in ball clay, or gum siccatives. Gases thus formed may result in pinholes and bubbles in the final glaze. In some cases, preservatives like formaldehyde will help. If washed, dried, and reground the same glaze may be used without difficulty.

This sculptural candelabra has a functional yet far more exciting form than the traditional concept. Terra cotta, 16 inches high. Kenneth M. Green.

CHAPTER 7

KILN STACKING AND FIRING

There are several precautions to be taken in stacking and loading a kiln. Although some procedures may seem unnecessary at times, nevertheless, for continued good results it is advisable to observe strictly the routine suggested below.

Stacking Procedures

Kiln stacking is usually easier if the pieces are first arranged and transferred on a loading table equipped with casters. Shelf supports can be used to determine the necessary height and shelf sizes can be marked out on the table. In this manner an entire kiln load can be planned out in advance. Planning on a table is a great help if the kiln is large or if it is a deep-front loader.

The kiln wash on the floor and upper surfaces of the shelves must be in good condition for a glaze fire. For firings which reach porcelain temperatures, a fresh coating of wash for each load is recommended. There are many protective kiln coatings on the market. An inexpensive wash can be made with equal parts by volume of kaolin and flint.

Check the elements if an electric kiln is used. After successive firings, the nickel-nichrome element wires of low-fire kilns tend to contract and to pull from the channel recesses. They may be carefully stretched and put back into place provided that they have not been made brittle by a firing over 2000° F. The coils of the wire should not touch each other or they will develop hot spots, which lessen the life of the element. Check old elements for breaks before each kiln loading. Be especially careful not to move Kanthal high-fire elements since they become very brittle and break easily after having been fired to cone 4 or above.

Thermocouple ends also become very brittle after successive firings. When the kiln is being loaded or unloaded, the shelves should not be allowed to touch them. The pieces and the shelves should not be placed closer than 1 inch from the thermocouple ends or the temperature reading will be inaccurate. While pyrometers are very convenient to use, they are not quite as accurate for ceramic purposes as pyrometric cones. The pyrometer measures the actual heat in the kiln, whereas the cone measures the work heat. Since the cone is composed of glaze materials, its reaction to heat is similar to that of the glaze. A long, slow rise in temperature will cause a chemical reaction to take place within the glaze at a lower temperature than if the heat rise is rapid. The difference in maturing points between a 108° F and a 270° F per-hour temperature rise is 18° F at cone 04 and 48° F at cone 8.

It is a good policy to check a pyrometer occasionally with a cone, especially when a new thermocouple is installed, since the new readings are likely to be different. There is a screw on the face of most pyrometers by which the indicated temperature can be adjusted to correspond to the result shown by the cone.

Check the foot rims of all glazed pots before loading the kiln to make certain that they are free of glaze. In addition, the glaze should be cleaned back at least ⅛ of an inch from the foot. Glazes which have runny tendencies should be applied thinner near the foot area. Charcoal, if rubbed on above the foot rim, will retard a runny glaze. In general, glazes of this type should either be fired at a lower temperature or have the R_2O_3 factor increased.

Loading distances will vary, depending upon whether the firing is for a bisque or a glaze. All wares must be placed at least 1 inch away from side walls containing heating muffles or elements. Large glazed bowls should be placed in the center of the kiln to reduce the possibility of warpage. Flat bisque bowls are best fired lying upside down on a flat shelf for the same reason. For a bisque fire the raw-ware bodies may touch each other. In fact, it is customary to stack bowls or similarly shaped vessels inside or over one another, provided that each one adequately supports the other. The problem in loading is to utilize, if possible, every available inch of space. Pieces are often placed upon shelf supports in order to occupy odd

This kiln load makes maximal use of the available space.

spaces that would otherwise be wasted. Furthermore, a kiln fires better if it is evenly stacked with a full load.

For a bright glaze the pieces should be ¼ inch apart. However, a greater distance is advisable for either a mat-glazed or a rough-textured piece unglazed on the exterior since a shine or color variation is likely to develop if these pieces are either too close to the heating surfaces or to another piece.

Shelf bottoms should be wiped off before they are placed into position. Waste particles from the kiln wash and from the insulating brick cling to them and if they remain, they will cause blemishes in the bowls beneath. A special top shelf is often desirable if the kiln has been in operation for any length of time. The constant expansion and contraction to which a kiln is exposed will in time cause the kiln bricks and cements to check and exfoliate particles of the brick. This is especially true of top-loading kiln covers and overhead brick muffles.

Shelf supports should serve to hold up the shelves adequately without taking up too much room. When there are several shelves, the center stilts can usually support two shelves. Large and thick shelves do not need center stilts. Shelves should always be level so that a glaze pool in a large bowl will not be off center, or so that a tall-necked piece will not be inclined to bend. Clay pads placed on shelf supports for leveling purposes should be of a high-fire type so they will not fuse to the shelf supports or the shelf.

This pot was heated too rapidly, and the thicker portion of its body exploded.

Firing Cycle

Firing a kiln is the final step in the rather long process of pottery making. A certain amount of care has to be exercised in order to obtain satisfactory results.

A preliminary heating with the kiln door open is necessary to remove the moisture which always remains in the ware at room temperatures. The heating time should be at least two hours for raw ware and longer for heavy pieces and ceramic sculpture. Heating raw ware too rapidly will cause the trapped water vapor to turn into steam. The expansions which necessarily accompany steam formation will cause the thicker portions of the clay to explode. Air bubbles in the clay, which are so often blamed for breakages, will usually cause trouble only if the clay is fired too rapidly. Never place slightly damp pieces in the kiln, regardless of the preheating period; accidents are more likely to happen when the potter tries to hurry up the normal drying process.

A gradual rise in temperature is preferable. During the firing cycle, the compounds composing the clay and glaze undergo numerous chemical changes, with resultant expansions and contractions. Best results can be obtained only if the temperature rise is gradual and uniform. Firing to cone 04 should take eight hours and in any case never less than six hours. Firing to cone 8 will usually take from eight to ten hours and with some kilns slightly longer. A kiln will have a longer useful life if the cooling-off time is at least double the firing time. It is especially important to cool off large pieces and sculpture slowly. Never crack the door of a kiln until the temperature is down to at least 400° F, and never open it fully or unload it until the temperature drops to 300° F.

Ceramic pyrometric cones have been mentioned briefly in comparison with pyrometers. They are small triangular pyramids composed of ceramic materials similar to glazes. Since the cones are calculated to bend and melt at specific intervals over a wide range of temperatures, they are available to suit just about every need. The most accurate method of using cones consists of using a group of three cones. For instance, if the desired temperature is cone 04, place a pad of clay with three cones reading 03, 04, and 05 in the kiln. When cone 05 melts, you will be alerted for the bending of cone 04 and you will be able to catch it in time. Cone 03 will indicate a heat rise beyond cone 04. In an electric kiln, the heat drops immediately when the current is cut off. Since heat tends to rise in an electric kiln, it may be necessary to turn the top controls to medium when the top cone melts. Leaving the bottom section on high will allow heat to build up in the lower part of the kiln. This is especially important if a shelf is placed near the bottom. In large gas kilns, however, the heat may rise slightly in some sections after the fuel has been turned off and the draft closed because greater heat is produced in the firebox and is soaked up into the chamber above. Actually the heat may not rise. The effect of holding a glaze at a given temperature for a longer period will automatically cause both the glaze and the cone to melt and flow at lower temperatures. (See the cone table in the Appendix. Note that the smaller-size cones react at slightly different temperatures.)

Mention might also be made of the use of cones in reduction firings. The regular cones in the lower fire ranges are red in color (from iron oxide). If used in a reduction fire, they react with the carbon and film over. Under these conditions the cones give an inaccurate reading. For reduction firings, therefore, specify the use for which the cones are intended. Low reduction-fire cones are white like those used in the higher fired ranges.

The formation of copper reds and celadons by reduction depends as much upon the correct atmosphere of the kiln as it does upon the compounding of the glaze. (See Reduction Glazes, Appendix.) Normally, the instructions for mixing reduction glazes also include directions for firing. In general the standard procedure is to use an *oxidizing fire* until it reaches a temperature just below that at which the first glaze ingredients melt. The temperature at which reduction will start may be anywhere from cone 016 to cone 1, depending upon the maturing point of the glaze. Reduction is

Tall bottles are most decorative and a challenge for the potter to throw. These stoneware bottles are 21 inches high. Stephen Polchirt.

caused by the presence of excess carbon in the kiln atmosphere, or, to phrase it in another way, by the absence of oxygen in the kiln chamber.

There are conflicting opinions concerning reduction firing in electric kilns. The makers of Kanthal wire, one of the major high-firing elements, advise against reduction firing as it may injure the elements. The general practice in an electric kiln is to use an artificial reduction with silicon carbide to obtain copper reds.

In a kiln burning gas, coal, oil, or wood, the usual procedure is to cut down the air intake or partly to close the chimney damper, thus causing an incomplete combustion which will form carbon monoxide. In a muffle kiln, the upper sections, or in a Denver kiln, a front tube, must be removed so that combustion gases can enter the kiln chamber. Since cutting down the air intake also reduces the heat, the fire must be shortly changed to an oxidizing fire so that the heat will continue to rise. This off-and-on reduction process is usually repeated several times during the firing. A number of cones should be employed and an accurate record of the firing kept since results for both color and texture will vary depending upon the initial time, length, and number of reducing intervals. Carbon can be introduced into the kiln chambers without lowering the temperature by inserting moth balls or fat pine splinters into the peep hole or through a special firing port. Often a combination of the two methods is used. Even artificial reductions work better if the general atmosphere is slightly reducing.

The reduction fire also has an effect upon the body, giving it a grayer color than normal and causing iron specks to darken and color the glaze. In fact, reduction firings are often used to alter body color and thereby the over-all effect of the glaze, and without any desire to obtain a copper-red or a celadon color. As a rule the strong reduction is seldom continued after cone 1, the remainder of the firing cycle being neutral or only slightly reducing. During the final cone or two an oxidizing atmosphere, which reputedly gives a better surface finish to the glaze, is generally employed.

A strong unaffected stoneware teapot in the
typical Bernard Leach tradition. Michael Cardew,
England. (Courtesy of *Pottery Quarterly*)

CHAPTER 8

CONTEMPORARY EUROPEAN CERAMICS

The title of this chapter is somewhat of a misnomer, but it is used for lack
of a better one. The size of this text does not permit a full treatment of
European ceramics. Instead, the discussion will be limited to the countries
with which I am most familiar and which incidentally have a culture and
living standard comparable to our own. Although this is not my chief
purpose, certain comparisons will be made, and these are valid only because social and economic conditions are roughly parallel.

The destructive influence of mass-production techniques was less prevalent
in Europe than in the United States. In most European countries the
various crafts continued to provide a livelihood for many artisans who, by
virtue of the apprenticeship system, passed on their skills to succeeding
generations. Except for a few isolated cases American handicrafts did not
survive industrialization, and a large group of those active today in
American crafts are of either European birth or European training.

The rise of large factories with mass-production methods placed cheaper
ware upon the market. But it also took the responsibility for design away
from the person best equipped to understand it, the potter, and gave it
to the factory manager and salesman whose chief criterion was profits.
European ceramics of the eighteenth and nineteenth centuries is particularly poor. While production methods were developed and research pro-
gressed to the point of enabling manufacturers to reproduce Oriental
porcelain, the designs were merely copies of Chinese, Greek, and Roman
ceramics. Unfortunately the models selected were usually the most ornate
pieces available.

(Top) A varied selection of bowls. Murray Fieldhouse, England. (Middle, left) Stoneware dish. Shoji Hamada, Japan. Hamada, an old friend of Bernard Leach, has spent considerable time in England. (Middle, right) Stoneware spice jar. Bernard Leach, England. (Bottom) Jar with the strong form generally associated with functional pieces. Bernard Leach, England. (Photos courtesy of *Pottery Quarterly*)

The pieces illustrated in this section are primarily from England and Scandinavia, with a few from Germany and Spain. At the time of World War I a number of small potteries were still functioning in various out-of-the-way sections of Europe. By and large these shops were producing utilitarian pieces for local consumption. However, the present rather considerable rebirth of ceramics is only in a very minor way due to the remnants of the old craft tradition. A more significant factor was the short-lived but revolutionary German Bauhaus movement. Its philosophy compelled a re-evaluation of design concepts and of the relationship between function and materials, and emphasized sensory and emotional reactions to art objects. This philosophy was quite a contrast to nineteenth-century design concepts which sprang primarily from literary themes and had various social and moral overtones. The contemporary European pieces illustrated in this chapter are representative of the type of work presently being done.

English Ceramics

For the few pottery students who have neither read his excellent pottery book nor seen his work displayed, a brief mention must first be made of Bernard Leach, the dean of English potters. Perhaps he more than any other person has influenced the direction of contemporary work in Great Britain. Mr. Leach was born in the Orient and educated in English schools, where his training emphasized art. As a young man he returned to the Far East and became interested in Japanese ceramics. So great was his enthusiasm that he apprenticed himself to a master potter and worked seriously with him for several years. After an absence of many years, Leach returned to England and set up a small pottery at St. Ives. Recognition came slowly but in time both the public and students discovered him. Many of England's better-known potters and several Americans have studied with Bernard Leach.

Mr. Leach's philosophy, naturally influenced by his long stay in the East, stresses complete mastery of the material, simplicity of form, and avoidance of unnecessary decoration. While confirming his belief in the craftsman as an artist, Mr. Leach does not sanction the concept of art for art's sake. He disapproves of the "exhibition" type of pottery and feels that the potter's work should be reasonably priced, functional, and available to the average man. The influence of this credo is evident on the following pages. By comparison, the pottery in the United States is more varied and more decorative, and perhaps as a result more pieces are priced out of reach of the average person's purse.

The pottery on this page was made by an English studio team. (Above) Coffee-set of an unusual design. Lucie Rie. (Below) Stoneware vases with textured slip and stain design. Hans Coper. (Courtesy of *Pottery Quarterly*)

(Top) Casseroles. Ladi Kwali, an African student of Michael Cardew.

(Bottom, left) Several pieces which do not conform to the usùal sedate English tradition. Rosemary Wren, England.

(Bottom, right) Plate with slip and sgraffito design. T. S. Haile, England.

(Photos coutesy of *Pottery Quarterly*)

Severe stoneware vase with slip or stain decoration. Rosemary Wren, England. (Courtesy of *Pottery Quarterly*)

Ceramic bird sculpture which suggests the alert and bobbing movements generally associated with fowl. Margaret Hine, England. (Courtesy of *Pottery Quarterly*)

Full potted form with incised decoration. Michael Cardew, England. (Courtesy of *Pottery Quarterly*)

A delicate bottle, illustrating the fallacy of thinking that all English pottery is severe. Waistrel Cooper, England. (Courtesy of *Pottery Quarterly*)

Bottle and vase, stamped decoration showing through an opaque glaze. Gutte Ericksen, Denmark. (*Den Permanente*)

Danish Ceramics

A comparison of Danish pottery with English pottery shows a similarity: both have a rather severe concept of form. However, the Danes seem to be more interested in decoration of various types.

With the exception of Saxbo ware which is produced in a small pottery employing about a dozen workers, the pieces shown here were all made in small individual workshops. Unlike the English and American potters who must market their own wares, the Danes have a fine display and market outlet (see p. 65). *Den Permanente* (the Permanent Exhibition of Danish Arts and Crafts) is a very remarkable display store in downtown Copenhagen, operated under a nonprofit charter. Its board of directors include, in addition to craftsmen, manufacturers, government officials, and art teachers. To maintain standards, a jury of craftsmen judge prospective entrants. Display and sales space is thus open to any Danish craftsman of ability. The potter has only to deliver his work to the shop and has no further responsibility for its sale. At present the work of more than 350 Danish craftsmen is on display. Although a few large firms are represented, on the whole the individual craftsman, working in a basement shop, dominates the exhibition. *Den Permanente*, which was started on a modest scale in 1931, has had a great effect upon Danish crafts generally. Not only does it provide Danish craftsmen with an outlet, but its success has encouraged other stores to carry better-designed merchandise, which has often meant handmade products.

Bowls and a freely thrown jar, hand-decorated and glaze trailed decoration. Lisa Engquist, Denmark. (*Den Permanente*)

Saxbo stoneware with their characteristically flawless mat glazes. Denmark. (*Den Permanente*)

Squat stoneware bottles, impressed designs under a gray-white glaze. Finn Lynggaard, Denmark. (*Den Permanente*)

(Top, left) A childhood fantasy, a girl with a big cat. Earthenware with incised and stain decoration, 18½ inches high. Finn Carlsen. (Top, right) Fine examples of freely executed slip and sgraffito decoration. Lisa Engquist. (Bottom, left) Stoneware bottle with pressed decorations. Christian Poulsen. (Bottom, right) Bowl with groggy textured body and impressed designs, Saxbo stoneware. Eva Staehr Nielsen. All pieces on this page from *Den Permanente*, Denmark.

The illustrated pieces show the variety of Danish decorative treatments. Equally interesting are many of the stoneware mat glazes, particularly those developed by Nathalie Krebs, the owner and manager of the Saxbo pottery and a very skilled glaze chemist as well. Mrs. Krebs insists on glaze perfection for every Saxbo piece and she destroys pieces whose glazes develop shines even in only one or two spots. Knowing this, it has been easier for me to break up some of my own pieces.

The possibilities of form seem to be endless. Wilhelm Käge, Gustavsberg, Sweden. (Photo Hilding Ohlson; courtesy of *Form* Magazine)

Swedish Ceramics

Here, for the first time in this text, several mass-produced items are shown. These are of sufficient merit to warrant inclusion. They represent the products of two of Sweden's largest ceramic concerns, Rörstand's and Gustavsberg's. It is interesting to note that in all Swedish advertising the name of the designer, as well as the manufacturer, is always mentioned. Perhaps this mention is indicative of the importance given to creative efforts in Sweden and may explain, in part, why Scandinavian design has in recent years captivated the world with its freshness.

The roots of so-called Swedish modern go back many years. Prior to World War I many of the private industries in Sweden had come under partial government ownership. These new owners were interested in producing quality products for the public. During exhibitions of European crafts and industrial-design products, they had noted, the Swedish entrants were not particularly outstanding. A crash program was devised. By invitation of the government a number of qualified younger artists were offered the art directorships of various semi-state-controlled industries. Among those so invited who are well known today were Edward Hald of Orrefors and Wilhelm Käge of Gustavsberg. At Gustavsberg, Käge not only learned the craft of the potter but also brought to it an artistic sensi-

(Top, left and right) Examples of Stig Lindberg's more recent studio designs. Compared to his earlier elongated graceful forms they seem rather cold. Gustavsberg Studio, Sweden. (Courtesy of *Form* Magazine).

(Bottom, left) Stoneware vases revealing characteristics typical of Käge: unusual forms, carved decorations, and contrasts between glazed and unglazed areas. Gustavsberg, Sweden. (Photo Hilding Ohlson; courtesy of *Form* Magazine)

tivity and a curiosity concerning the great ceramic periods of the past, notably the Chinese and Persian. Echoes of these periods appear in his work but Käge translated these echoes into a very personal statement. Käge's protégé and successor at Gustavsberg, Stig Lindberg, has continued to guide factory production while personally developing a series of streamlined forms which have been copied everywhere.

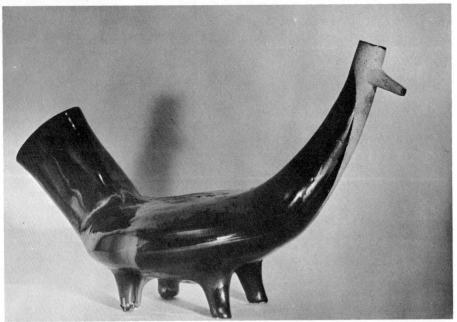

(Top, left) These functional ovenware forms designed for factory production seem at first glance quite a contrast to the other Lindberg pieces shown.   But take another look. Gustavsberg, Sweden. (Top, right, and bottom) Sculptural flower vases by one of Sweden's younger independent potters, revealing an approach more whimsical than that of established potters. The woman is brown stoneware; the bird, yellow-clay stoneware, finished with a brown-blue glaze. Gunilla Palmstierna. (Photos courtesy of *Form* Magazine)

(Top, left) Mass-produced functional stoneware pieces. Carl-Harry Stälhane, Rörstrand, Sweden.

(Top, right) Tea set. Marianne Westman, Rörstrand, Sweden.

(Bottom, right) Coffee set of thin porcelain. Louise Adelborg, Rörstrand, Sweden.

(Photos courtesy of *Form* Magazine)

A number of smaller potteries and individual workshops are operating in Sweden as in Denmark but they seem to be overshadowed by their larger competitors. Gunilla Palmstierna, whose decorative sculptural pieces are illustrated, is typical of the younger potters who are interested in more whimsical and less functional pieces.

Bottle forms. Okki Laine, Arabia Studios, Finland.

Finnish Ceramics

Culturally Finland is one of the Scandinavian countries, but politically it is precariously squeezed in between Sweden and Russia. Morally a victor in its 1939 war with Russia, Finland has had economic difficulties ever since. The spirit of its struggle has apparently carried over into the private lives of its citizens, and there has been a design revival of considerable significance. In such fields as architecture, furniture, glass, textiles, silver, and ceramics, the quality of work presently being produced is all out of proportion to the size of the Finnish population and other such expectancy factors.

The moving factor in Finnish ceramics is the giant Arabia factory. It has many unusual features. Of chief interest to the potter is the large studio section maintained by the factory. On the top floor of an eight-story building are about a dozen studios overlooking the Helsinki bay and countryside. All the ceramics illustrated in this section were executed by members of this studio group, with the exception of those by Kaj Franck, the art director of factory production work and a noted glass designer as well. While the studio members are on a monthly payroll, they are, for the most part, entirely free to work in whatever direction interests them. Thus, some make functional pieces and others, purely decorative ceramics. One or two, like Rut Bryk, have an entirely two-dimensional painterlike approach. Michael Schilkin, on the other hand, is basically a sculptor working in a ceramic medium. The pieces produced in this studio are displayed

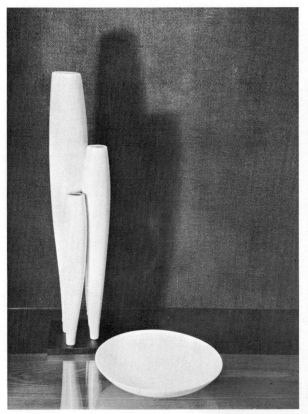

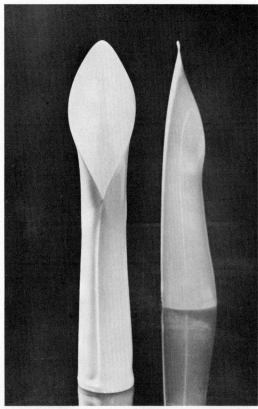

(Top, left) Porcelain bowl and cylindrical vases. Friedl Kjellberg, Arabia Studios, Finland.

(Top, right, and bottom) Glasslike decorative bowls and vases of eggshell-thin porcelain, made in molds. Aune Siimes, Arabia Studios, Finland.

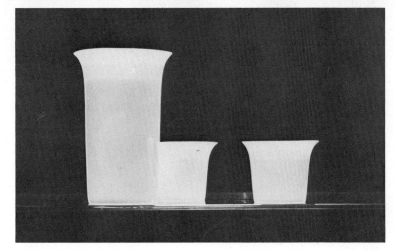

and sold in a shop in downtown Helsinki. In addition, these ceramics are sent to various international exhibitions where they have received numerous awards. As award winners, they enhance not only the individual's reputation but that of the factory which the craftsman represents.

(Top, left) A forceful, well-potted stoneware pitcher. Kyllikki Salmenhaara. (Top, right) Mugs exhibiting a truly clay feeling. Marjukka Paasivirta. (Bottom, left) A variety of ovenware pieces. Kaj Franck. (Bottom, right) Intriguing bottle forms. Francesca Lindh. All pieces on this page from Arabia Studios, Finland.

The existence of such a prestige group naturally creates a problem for younger ceramists. While there is a certain turnover of personnel, most studio members have remained at the Arabia studio for many years. Any new members are generally selected from promising students at the Art Academy who have perhaps served an apprenticeship in a smaller shop.

(Top, left) An elongated thrown sphere skillfully converted into a walrus. Michael Schilkin. (Top, right) A ceramic plaque. Rut Bryk. (Middle) Avant-garde ceramic sculpture. Oiva Toikka. (Bottom) Stoneware teapots and hot-water containers in unusual combination. Richard Lindh. All pieces on this page from Arabia Studios, Finland.

Unusual stoneware bottle form and bowl with a beautifully textured mat glaze. Antonio Serret, Barcelona, Spain.

Other European Ceramics

Naturally a craft as widespread as ceramics will have followers everywhere. Space does not permit an over-all survey. Work of interest is being done throughout the world, and influences of both a regional and an international character can often be detected. The last pieces illustrated here are from Spain and Germany. Individually they are of interest, but without a large sampling no conclusions as to a national trend can be formed.

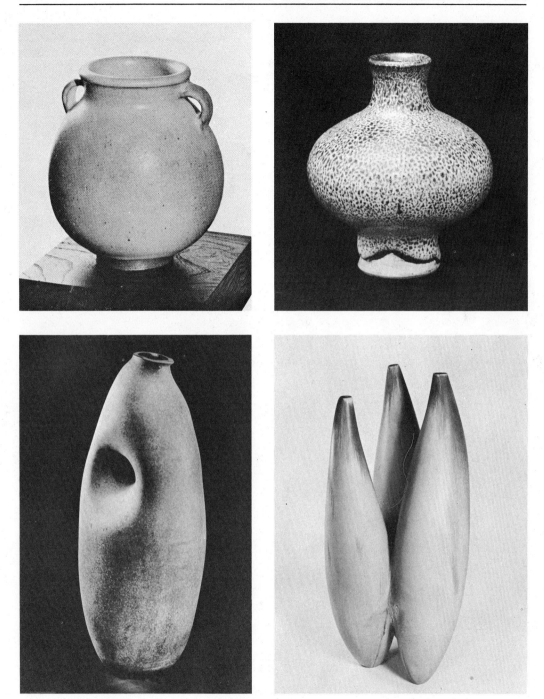

(Top, left) Stoneware jar suggestive of Grecian forms. (Top, right) Unusual bottle form. Both pieces by Jan Bontjes van Beek, West Berlin, Germany. (Bottom, left) Large stoneware bottle. The depression serves as a unique handle. (Bottom, right) An interesting cluster of bottle forms with mat glazes. Both pieces by Richard Bampi, Kandern, Germany.

The finger ridges left on this beautifully potted
vase merge decoration with form. Freely brushed
wax resist and iron sulfate over a dolomite glaze.
Harvey Littleton. (Kunstman Studio)

CHAPTER 9

CERAMIC CALCULATIONS

Thus far this text has covered in a general manner clays, glazes, and decorating methods. From time to time mention was made of the ceramic
chemicals involved. I did not wish to complicate matters by discussing
the chemical makeup of glazes when the student was trying to learn many
new terms and techniques. However, it cannot be avoided entirely if we
are to understand and control the medium.

Most students and many potters think that glaze calculations and glaze
chemistry are extremely difficult. This is not true, at least not at the ele-
mentary, theoretical level sufficient for studio ceramics. To develop a
working knowledge of glaze chemistry, no previous training in chemistry
is necessary, and likewise, a grammar-school proficiency in arithmetic is
adequate for working out all the glaze calculations encountered here.
Previous training in chemistry is of secondary importance because ceramic
chemistry is primarily concerned with silicate chemistry, a subject barely
mentioned in survey courses in chemistry.

The all-important compound is silicon dioxide, commonly called *silica*.
In *chemical terms*, silica is expressed by the symbols, SiO_2, which is also the
molecular formula for silica. The oxide form is stable at all normal temperatures and consists of one atom of silicon combined with two atoms of
oxygen. Over one hundred different kinds of atoms have been discovered
in the earth's surface. They all have differing weights. (See the Appendix.)
The lightest of the elements, hydrogen, formerly was given a unit of one,
and all other elements were given weights in relationship to it. However,
as experiments became more accurate, hydrogen was found to have a

weight of 1.008. At present, oxygen, with an atomic weight of 16, is taken as the unit of comparison. Oxygen and silicon are the elements most frequently found in ceramic materials.

To find the molecular weight of a compound we must first know the molecular formula and the *atomic weights* of its constituent elements. The formula for silica is SiO_2. From the atomic table in the Appendix, we find that the weight of silica is 28.06. Since the atomic weight of oxygen is 16, two atoms of oxygen would weigh 32. This, plus 28.06, gives a molecular weight of 60.06 for the compound silica. For ease in calculating, this figure is generally written as 60.1 or even 60.

Pure silica or rock crystal is remarkably hard and transparent. It is also a beautiful material. The ease with which silica combines under the influence of heat with the alkaline earths and low-melting metallic oxides to form a variety of glassy substances is the phenomenon which makes not only glazes but ceramics, as a whole, possible. Our entire study of glazes and clay bodies is almost exclusively concerned with this problem: the union of silica and other compounds. In order that we understand clearly the materials with which our calculations are concerned, we should first review briefly some of the information mentioned earlier in the sections on clays and glazes.

What is clay? Clays are formed by the gradual weathering, over millions of years, of pegmatite-type rocks, such as granite. Occasionally, clay may be found on the original location of the parent rock, as in Cornwall, England, or in the residual kaolin deposits in North Carolina. But often the clay has been moved by wind or water from its original site. Some such sedimentary clay deposits, like the kaolin beds in Georgia and Florida, are remarkably clean, but, in general, sedimentary clays contain many mineral impurities and some organic matter. Too much organic matter will result in the excessive shrinkage of manufactured clay products. Coarse sand will cut the plasticity of the clay to such an extent that it may be impossible to shape a vessel. Additional minerals may have the effect of either raising maturing temperatures to an impractical degree or causing deformation at moderately low temperatures.

Pure clay has the formula $Al_2O_3 \cdot 2SiO_2 \cdot 2H_2O$. By weight, pure clay, also called *kaolin* or *china clay*, has the following composition:

Formula	Composition	
$Al_2O_3 \cdot 2SiO_2 \cdot 2H_2O$	Alumina	39.45%
	Silica	46.64
	Water	13.91

The average clay will contain from 50 to 70 percent of this pure clay substance. The balance will be made up of compounds of iron, calcium, potash, sodium, magnesium, titanium, and minute quantities of other minerals. These proportions will vary from one clay deposit to another and will markedly affect the working, as well as the firing, qualities of the particular clay in question. Clays have been classified into several types having definite characteristics, such as earthenware, fire clay, stoneware clay, and so forth. For the most part, each compound found in a clay body contributes a special quality to it. In most cases the effect is roughly comparable whether the material is in a clay or a glaze. A glance at the next chapter dealing with ceramic materials might be helpful to get an idea of some of the compounds found in glazes and clay bodies. The function of these various compounds may be understood better if we briefly describe what happens to clay during the firing process.

Firing changes in a clay body are extremely important and must be understood if we are to learn how to make additions to improve a body or to alter its maturing temperature. In the firing of an earthenware body, the atmospheric water vapor will begin to leave it at 400° F. As the heat reaches 900° F, some of the water which is combined chemically will begin to leave the body. By 1300° F (a red heat) all such water should have left the body. Shortly after this, the first appreciable shrinkage of the body should occur. During this same period organic matter in the clay will burn out. Low-firing clays contain impurities in the form of the carbonates or sulfates of calcium, magnesium, and iron. At the red heat these compounds decompose and give off a gas in the form of carbon dioxide, or sulphur dioxide. The inability of these gases to escape through the glaze may be responsible for such glaze defects as pinholes and blisters. Iron and other low-melting compounds in earthenware will begin to combine with silica found in the various clay minerals to form a glassy bond. Between 1750° and 1850° F silica combines with alumina to form interlocking needlelike crystals of great strength, called mullite. Due to the low-melting fluxes contained in earthenware bodies, they usually cannot be fired over 2000° F without being seriously deformed. The earthenware body, although mature at 1850° F, is still quite porous and in comparison with stoneware, it is rather fragile. The firing of a stoneware or porcelain body is roughly similar to that of earthenware. The difference is that, lacking low-melting fluxes, the silica compounds break down and fuse at a higher temperature. Due to the greater amounts of alumina in the body, the ware does not deform easily and the silica is allowed to flow into all the pores, resulting in a completely vitrified body at 2300° to 2500° F.

Firing changes in a glaze are roughly similar to those of a clay body. It is primarily a matter of the fluxes involved. Many clay bodies, if fired at very high temperatures, will become fluid enough to flow as a glaze and upon cooling, will form a glassy state like a glaze. (See Slip Glazes.) All clays and glazes contain what we call fluxes. A *flux* may be either a low-melting metallic oxide such as lead, iron, lithium, or sodium or an alkaline earth compound of lime or magnesia. In the firing cycle, these fluxes first melt and readily combine with silica. Silica, if fired alone, has the extremely high melting point of 3119° F, but if combined with a large amount of low-firing fluxes, silica will develop a glassy state as low as 1100° F. The part played by silica in a glaze is that of a *glass former*. The development of mullite crystals from silica and alumina was mentioned before. Alumina, like silica, is another high-melting material (3277° F) which can be induced to form new chemical combinations due to the actions of the lower-melting fluxes. In a glaze or body, alumina functions as a *refractory*. It resists the deforming action of high temperatures and provides the stable structure of the glaze and body. Alumina reacts slowly to the action of the fluxes but combines with silica to form tough crystalline forms interlocking the body and the glaze.

The RO, R$_2$O$_3$, RO$_2$ System

In the previous section we briefly discussed some of the characteristics of glazes. In particular, it was noted that all glazes consisted of three primary parts: a flux, a refractory element, and a glass former. A great deal of study has gone into the chemistry of glazes. The first purpose of any study is to find out all the information about the field. Of equal importance is the arrangement of this material into some sort of system by which the parts can be related to the whole. By isolating specific chemicals in the glaze, experiments have revealed the part played by each material. It was in this manner that certain ingredients were found to have either a fluxing, refractory, or glass-forming effect in the glaze.

The RO, R$_2$O$_3$, and the RO$_2$ system is based upon the separation of the component oxides of the various ceramic materials into one of the three major parts of a glaze formula. It was observed that the oxides playing a particular role in the glaze had, for the most part, a similar chemical arrangement. The symbol RO is merely a substitution for a metallic or alkaline element which forms its oxide by combining with one atom of oxygen such as CaO or PbO. In a like manner, alumina (Al$_2$O$_3$) may be symbolized by R$_2$O$_3$ and silica (SiO$_2$) by RO$_2$. A table may better illustrate this division of the component parts of a glaze.

Bases	Neutrals	Acids
Li_2O*	(Amphoteric oxides)	SiO_2
Na_2O*	Al_2O_3	TiO_2
K_2O*	B_2O_3	ZrO_2
CaO	Fe_2O_3	
MgO	Sb_2O_3	Glass formers
BaO	Cr_2O_3	
ZnO		
FeO		
MnO	Refractory elements	
PbO		
CdO		
Fluxing agents		

Bases · *Neutrals* (Amphoteric oxides) · *Acids*

Li_2O* · Na_2O* · K_2O* · CaO · MgO · BaO · ZnO · FeO · MnO · PbO · CdO — *Fluxing agents*

Al_2O_3 · B_2O_3 · Fe_2O_3 · Sb_2O_3 · Cr_2O_3 — *Refractory elements*

SiO_2 · TiO_2 · ZrO_2 — *Glass formers*

* One of the few exceptions; 2 atoms of sodium or potassium unite with 1 of oxygen to form the oxide.

In the first column are the RO oxides which have the effect of fluxes in either a glaze or a body. They are also called the *base oxides*. The elements in second column are not as easy to classify. Some of the *neutrals* or amphoteric oxides may on occasion function as either a base or an acid oxide. However, the major oxide in this group, alumina (Al_2O_3), always has a refractory effect in a glaze. On the other hand, red iron oxide (Fe_2O_3) is an active flux as well as a colorant. Boric acid (B_2O_3) can react either as a base or an acid. Silica is the major oxide in the acid column. The value of both TiO_2 and ZrO_2 in a glaze is for their opacity rather than for their glass-forming effect. The exceptions to these general divisions are rather minor. In practice the RO, R_2O_3, and RO_2 method of categorizing the main components of a glaze works very well.

The Empirical Glaze Formula

Largely for the purposes of comparison or as an aid to further calculations, glaze batches are usually reduced to an empirical formula. The *empirical formula* is a glaze formula in which the various active ingredients are expressed in molecular proportions. By contrast, the *batch recipe* is a proportion expressed by the actual weights of the raw chemical compounds making up the glaze. Since the materials used in the average glaze batch are rather complex compounds, it is a distinct advantage to be able to define the glaze in terms of single oxides which bear the same proportional relationship to each other as when in their more complex form in the glaze batch. These oxides are grouped into RO, R_2O_3, and RO_2 units.

A typical low-fire glaze formula is as follows:

RO	R$_2$O$_3$	RO$_2$
0.40 Na$_2$O	0.03 Al$_2$O$_3$	2.1 SiO$_2$
0.46 PbO	0.32 B$_2$O$_3$	
0.14 FeO		

It will be noticed that the RO group adds up to a unit of 1. This is not an accident. The relationship of the RO to the R$_2$O$_3$ or the RO$_2$ is very critical in glaze calculations. Comparisons cannot be made between glazes unless some standard exists. If, in converting from a batch to a formula, the RO does not total 1, then each number in the formula must be divided by the sum of the RO. This will bring the RO to a unity of 1, and the R$_2$O$_3$ and RO$_2$ will still have their same relative proportions.

The above formula is an extremely clear and concise way to state a glaze. In this form, comparisons can be made readily. Pure oxides, such as shown in the formula, are seldom found in nature. For economy purposes, glazes are made instead from standard mineral compounds. A glaze made from the above formula would need the exact amounts of the chemical compounds as listed below.

BATCH 1

Grams	Raw compound	Molecular formula
15.72	soda feldspar	Na$_2$O·Al$_2$O·6SiO$_2$
61.12	borax	Na$_2$O·2B$_2$O$_3$·10H$_2$O
22.26	soda ash	Na$_2$CO$_3$
118.58	white lead	2PbCO$_3$·Pb(OH)$_2$
11.20	red iron oxide	Fe$_2$O$_3$
114.60	silica	SiO$_2$

Another glaze batch using different raw materials but containing the same oxides in the same proportions as the original formula can be made as follows:

BATCH 2

Grams	Raw compound	Molecular formula
61.12	borax	Na$_2$O·2B$_2$O$_3$·10H$_2$O
25.44	soda ash	Na$_2$CO$_3$
104.89	red lead	Pb$_3$O$_4$
10.08	black iron oxide	FeO
7.74	kaolin	Al$_2$O$_3$·2SiO$_2$·2H$_2$O
122.4	silica	SiO$_2$

A glance at the figures in the two batches reveals that only in one case did the amounts of the raw materials remain the same. Three compounds used in Batch 1 are not used in Batch 2. Likewise, three ingredients not in Batch 1 are found in the second glaze. Although these two glazes are made in part from different compounds, they are chemically identical. This emphasizes the need to convert all glaze batches into formula form before trying to make valid comparisons or conclusions concerning the effect of individual oxides in the glaze.

The Batch Recipe

In the previous section the gram weights of the various compounds are given in decimal fractions because they have been exactly converted from the empirical formula. It is the usual practice to weigh out a larger amount of the glaze chemicals than shown above. In this case, the fractions are not important. But small test batches must be compounded very carefully to be of value. A *batch recipe* always consists of the raw compounds used to form the glaze with their weights given in grams, ounces, and so on. The maturing temperature should also be included.

Before a batch recipe is converted to an empirical formula, it is first necessary to know the chemical formulas of the individual raw materials as well as their equivalent weights. The molecular formulas and equivalent weights of the molecular components for all commonly used ceramic materials are listed in the Appendix. The table lists the common commercial name of the raw material in the first column and its molecular formula in the second column. Many compounds are designated by more than one name in common use, names which are often dissimilar as, for example, whiting and calcium carbonate.

Early in this chapter the *molecular weight of a compound* was defined as the sum of the atomic weights of its constituent elements. In the table on Raw Materials (Appendix), equivalent weights are listed for the RO, R_2O_3, and RO_2 groups. This listing is for convenience in calculations as will be seen shortly. The equivalent weight will often be the same as the molecular weight of the compound, but in many cases it will be smaller. This, too, is for ease in calculation. Take, for example, potash feldspar:

Raw material	Formula	Molecular weight	Equivalent weights RO	R_2O_3	RO_2
Feldspar (potash)	$K_2O \cdot Al_2O_3 \cdot 6SiO_2$	556.8	556.8	556.8	92.9

According to the given formula, when one molecular unit of potash feld-spar is added, the glaze will have one unit of potassium oxide, one unit of alumina, and six units of silica. Since one unit each of potassium oxide and alumina form the compound, their individual equivalent weights are 556.8. Since six units of silica are necessary to form the compound, the equivalent weight of silica is $\frac{1}{6}$ of the compound weight, or 92.9. The *equivalent weights* of the oxides of a compound are the same as its molecular weight if the oxide in question appears only once. If more than one unit of an oxide occurs, then its equivalent weight will be found by dividing the compound molecular weight by the number of times the oxide in question appears.

These definitions will become clearer in the actual procedure of converting the following glaze batch recipe to an empirical formula.

Glaze recipe	Raw materials	Parts by weight
A lead-borax	white lead	128
glaze ma-	whiting	15
turing at	borax	103
cone 04	feldspar (potash)	83
	kaolin	38
	flint	85

Before we can go into the actual calculations, we must first find the molecular formula of each of the compounds making up the glaze, plus the equivalent weights of the oxides contained in these compounds. It is convenient to put this information in the form of a table (opposite page). By checking over the raw-material formulas, we can determine which of the oxides need to be indicated in the spaces to the right of the table.

The batch weights of the raw materials are divided by the equivalent molecular weights of the particular oxides concerned, giving the molecular proportions in the form of single oxides. By arranging these oxides with the amounts calculated into RO, R_2O_3, and RO_2 groups, we find that the glaze batch has the following empirical formula:

RO	R_2O_3	RO_2
.495 PbO	.295 Al_2O_3	2.599 SiO_2
.150 CaO	.540 B_2O_3	
.149 K_2O		
.270 Na_2O		

The total of the RO oxides comes to 1.064 instead of the desired unit of

BATCH TO EMPIRICAL FORMULA

Raw material and formula	Batch weights		Equivalent weights		PbO	CaO	Na₂O	B₂O₃	K₂O	Al₂O₃	SiO₂
White lead (2PbCO₃·Pb(OH)₂)	128	÷	(RO) 258.5	=	.495						
Whiting (CaCO₃)	15	÷	(RO) 100	=		.15					
Borax (Na₂O·2B₂O₃·10H₂O)	103	÷	(RO) 381.04 (R₂O₃) 190.7	=			.270	.540			
Feldspar (potash) (K₂O·Al₂O₃·6SiO₂)	83	÷	(RO) 556.8 (R₂O₃) 556.8 (RO₂) 92.9	=					.149	.149	.89
Kaolin (Al₂O₃·2SiO₂·2H₂O)	38	÷	(R₂O₃) 258.1 (RO₂) 129.	=						.146	.294
Flint (SiO₂)	85	÷	(RO₂) 60.06	=							1.415
Totals	452				.495	.15	.270	.540	.149	.295	2.599

one because round numbers have been used in the batch recipe. By dividing each of the above figures by 1.064 we will have the following empirical formula. The RO is now .998, a figure which is accurate enough for comparative purposes.

RO	R_2O_3	RO_2
.465 PbO	.277 Al_2O_3	2.442 SiO_2
.140 CaO	.507 B_2O_3	
.140 K_2O		
.253 Na_2O		

A ceramicist who does any glaze experimentation will have to make numerous calculations like the above. With reasonable care in selecting the equivalent weights he should have no trouble. Glaze experimentation is not like cooking; a pinch of this or that cannot be added indiscriminately. Considerable research has been done on the properties of ceramic materials and reasonable predictions may be made about the probable change that a particular chemical will cause in a known type of glaze. There are, however, many variable factors such as the length of the glaze grinding time, the thickness of its application, the reactions between glaze and body, the kiln atmosphere, and the rate of temperature rise or fall. Since each or all of these conditions may markedly affect a particular glaze, glaze experimentation is something less than a true science. Successful work largely depends upon the over-all experience and care of the operator in controlling these variables.

Since glazes can only be compared accurately in the empirical formulae form, glazes listed in the more technical ceramic books and magazines will be in this form. Therefore, they will have to be converted to a batch recipe before being used.

To convert an empirical formula to a batch recipe we have to reverse the procedure explained in the above section. Again, we must lay out a chart form on which to compile our information. This type of conversion will require a slightly greater familiarity with raw chemical compounds because we have to select those compounds containing the proper oxides without adding any unwanted elements. The parts of compounds which pass off in the kiln as gases or water vapor are ignored. To make the process clearer let us take the following *empirical glaze formula* and convert it into a batch recipe.

0.40 Na_2O	0.03 Al_2O_3	2.1 SiO_2
0.46 PbO	0.32 B_2O_3	
0.14 FeO		

CALCULATIONS FROM FORMULA TO BATCH RECIPE

		Na_2O	PbO	FeO	Al_2O_3	B_2O_3	SiO_2
Oxides in formula	*Equivalents needed*	0.40	0.46	0.14	0.03	0.32	2.1
Raw material	*Equivalents needed*						
Soda feldspar ($Na_2O \cdot Al_2O_3 \cdot 6SiO_2$)							
0.03 equivalents		0.03			0.03		0.18
	remainder	0.37	0.46	0.14		0.32	1.92
Borax ($Na_2O \cdot 2B_2O_3 \cdot 10H_2O$)							
0.16 equivalents		0.16				0.32	
	remainder	0.21	0.46	0.14			1.92
Soda ash (Na_2CO_3)							
0.21 equivalents		0.21					
	remainder		0.46	0.14			1.92
White lead ($2PbCO_3 \cdot Pb(OH)_2$)							
0.153 equivalents			0.46				
	remainder			0.14			1.92
Red iron oxide (Fe_2O_3)							
0.07 equivalents				0.14			
	remainder						1.92
Flint (SiO_2)							
1.92 equivalents							1.92

The general procedure is as follows: First, if any alkaline fluxes are present (Na_2O or K_2O), try to include as much as possible in a soda or potash feldspar. It is a cheaper source of the flux and, equally as important, it is nonsoluble and not as likely to lump up in a glaze like borax. Then fill out the other single oxides. Try to save the alumina for next to the last and take out the silica at the end. Alumina and silica are often included in other compounds and the balance can easily be taken care of last as either kaolin or silica. Since the silica is always in a larger amount than the alumina and is available in a cheap pure form, save it for the last item.

Several of the calculations on page 125 may seem incorrect at first so perhaps we should point out a few of these seeming inconsistencies. In the first addition, when we take 0.03 equivalents of soda feldspar, we get six times as much SiO_2 as either Na_2 or Al_2O_3 because the formula for soda feldspar is $Na_2O_3 \cdot Al_2O_3 \cdot 6SiO_2$. Similarly borax has twice as much B_2O_3 as Na_2O.

Now that we have the needed molecular equivalents of the chemical compounds, we can find the gram batch weights (or pounds) by multiplying each equivalent by the molecular weights of the chemical compound. Thus we get the following:

Raw material	Equivalents		Molecular weights		Batch weights
Soda feldspar	0.03	×	524	=	15.72
Borax	0.16	×	382	=	61.12
Soda ash	0.21	×	106	=	22.26
White lead	0.153	×	775	=	118.58
Red iron oxide	0.07	×	160	=	11.20
Flint	1.91	×	60	=	114.60

As noted before, it is possible for two apparently different glaze batches to be chemically identical. To illustrate this we can work out the last formula in a different fashion by obtaining alumina from kaolin and eliminating soda feldspar by using a larger proportion of soda ash. Other materials will also be changed. (See the table on p. 127. The recipe for Batch 2 uses the raw materials and weights listed below.)

Raw material	Equivalents		Molecular weights		Batch weights
Borax	0.16	×	382	=	61.12
Soda ash	0.24	×	106	=	25.44
Red lead	0.153	×	685	=	104.80
Black iron oxide	0.14	×	72	=	10.08
Kaolin	0.03	×	258	=	7.74
Flint	2.04	×	60	=	122.40

CALCULATIONS FROM FORMULA TO BATCH RECIPE 2

	Oxides in formula	Na_2O	PbO	FeO	Al_2O_3	B_2O_3	SiO_2
Raw material	Equivalents needed	0.40	0.46	0.14	0.03	0.32	2.1

Borax $(Na_2O_3 \cdot 2B_2O_3 \cdot 10H_2O)$

		Na_2O	PbO	FeO	Al_2O_3	B_2O_3	SiO_2
0.16 equivalents		0.16				0.32	
	remainder	0.24	0.46	0.14	0.03		2.1

Soda ash (Na_2CO_3)

0.24 equivalents		0.24					
	remainder		0.46	0.14	0.03		2.1

Red lead (Pb_3O_4)

0.153 equivalents			0.46				
	remainder			0.14	0.03		2.1

Black iron oxide   (FeO)

0.14 equivalents				0.14			
	remainder				0.03		2.1

Kaolin $(Al_2O_3 \cdot 2SiO_2 \cdot 2H_2O)$

0.03 equivalents					0.03		0.06
	remainder						2.04

Flint (SiO_2)

2.04 equivalents							2.04

As the comparative figures below show, the only item which has remained the same in the two recipes is the borax. Nevertheless each recipe is identical chemically and should give the same results in a glaze. The choice of raw materials depend upon availability, cost, and physical qualities such as adherence and shrinkage.

	BATCH 1	BATCH 2
Soda feldspar	15.72	none
Borax	61.12	61.12
Soda ash	22.26	25.44
White lead	118.58	none
Red lead	none	104.80
Red iron oxide	11.20	none
Black iron oxide	none	10.08
Flint	114.60	122.40
Kaolin	none	7.74

This unusual ceramic sculpture is really a pot.
An interesting combination of thrown forms and
textured surfaces, 35 inches high, it is decorated
with cobalt, iron, copper, and chrome oxides.
Henry Takemoto.

CHAPTER 10

CERAMIC CHEMICALS

In the previous section we stressed the ease with which glazes could be
compared with one another by reducing each one to its empirical formula.
This comparison, however, must be made with a certain amount of caution
since materials used in ceramic glazes are seldom pure oxides but often
complex mixtures, occasionally containing impurities not indicated in the
molecular formula. Therefore, when unexpected variations occur, the
purity of the materials should be considered. Raw materials may vary
slightly in composition from dealer to dealer, depending upon the refining
process and the original source. Ceramic raw materials are a large and
varied group of chemicals, which can be studied from many aspects, but as
we are interested in them as sources of the particular oxides needed in the
empirical glaze formula, it will probably be of most value to separate some
of the most frequently used items into the RO, R_2O_3, and RO_2 groups.
As will be seen, many are compounds, the individual parts of which may be
separated into two or three groups. Later in the chapter the compounds
will be described in more detail in an alphabetized listing.

Sources of Base (RO) Oxides

SODIUM (Na_2O) is one of the more common low-fire fluxes. It has the
highest coefficient of expansion of all the bases and generally gives a lower
tensile strength and elasticity to the silicates formed than most other fluxes.
The usual ceramic sources of sodium are as follows:

Sodium chloride (NaC)
Sodium carbonate (Na_2CO_3), more frequently called soda ash
Borax ($Na_2O \cdot 2B_2O_3 \cdot 10H_2O$)
Soda feldspar ($Na_2O \cdot Al_2O_3 \cdot 6SiO_2$)
Cryolite (Na_3AlF_6)

POTASSIUM (K_2O) is similar in fluxing action to sodium. It is generally more expensive but has the added advantages of having a lower coefficient of thermal expansion, increasing the hardness and brilliance of a piece, and lowering the fluidity of the glaze. Sources of potassium are:

Potassium carbonate (K_2CO_3), more commonly known as pearl ash

Potash feldspar ($K_2O \cdot Al_2O_3 \cdot 6SiO_2$)

Cornwall stone, a complex mixture with a ceramic formula of:

0.63 KNaO	1.3497 Al_2O_3	10.1127 SiO_2
0.32 CaO	0.0181 Fe_2O_3	0.785 H_2O
0.05 MgO		

Carolina stone, a domestic product similar to Cornwall stone

Volcanic ash, with a ceramic formula of:

0.660 K_2O	0.899 Al_2O_3	9.59 SiO_2
0.230 Na_2O	0.060 Fe_2O_3	0.05 TiO_2
0.096 CaO		
0.014 MgO		

LITHIUM (Li_2O) is more commonly used by glass manufacturers but it has several important qualities which make its occasional use in glazes valuable. Lithium (the oxide or carbonate) is expensive because of the small amounts of Li_2O (3 to 8 percent) found in the producing ores. It has a much lower atomic weight than either sodium or potassium (ratio of 1 to 3 and 1 to 5), and therefore a smaller amount of material can be used without lessening the fluxing action. This has the effect of decreasing tensions evolving from thermal expansions and contractions and therefore promoting a more durable glaze. Sources of lithium are:

Lepidolite ($LiF \cdot KF \cdot Al_2O_3 \cdot 3SiO_2$)

Spodumene ($Li_2O \cdot Al_2O_3 \cdot 4SiO_2$)

Lithium carbonate ($LiCO_3$)

CALCIUM (CaO) oxide, in comparison with the alkaline oxides just mentioned, produces a glaze more resistant to abrasion, mild acids, and weathering. It likewise lowers the coefficient of thermal expansion, therefore increasing the tensile strength. Although it is often used in small amounts with other fluxes in low-fire glazes, calcium should not be used as the sole flux at temperatures under cone 3. It is the most common flux used at porcelain temperatures. As with alumina, an excess of calcia tends to produce mat textures. Sources of calcium are:

Calcium carbonate ($CaCO_3$)

Calcium borate ($2CaO \cdot 3B_2O_3 \cdot 5H_2O$), more commonly known as colemanite

Dolomite [$CaMg (CO_3)_2$]

Calcium fluoride (CaF_2), better known as the mineral fluorspar

MAGNESIUM (MgO) is frequently found combined with the feldspars and limestones. It lowers the thermal expansion more than other bases and is as satisfactory as the alkaline fluxes in developing a durable glaze. In some combinations it will develop a slight opacity. Used with low-fired glazes magnesium has a refractory effect, but it fluxes easily at higher temperatures and becomes quite fluid. Sources of magnesium are:

Magnesium carbonate ($MgCO_3$)

Dolomite [$CaMg(CO_3)_2$]

Talc (varies from $3MgO \cdot 4SiO_2 \cdot H_2O$ to $4MgO \cdot 5SiO_2 \cdot H_2O$). In the solid and more impure form it is also known as steatite and soapstone.

BARIUM (BaO) is a very active flux under some conditions. Its glass formation has a brilliancy second only to the lead silicates. Barium's effect on the thermal expansion of the glaze is less than that of the alkalies and calcia.

Barium carbonate ($BaCO_3$)

ZINC (ZnO) can contribute several different factors to a glaze. It can be used to replace some of the more soluble alkaline fluxes. Zinc is second only to magnesium in reducing the thermal expansion and to calcium in increasing the strength and resistance of a glaze. It contributes some opacity to the glaze and is helpful in reducing crazing defects.

Zinc oxide (ZnO), the major zinc compound used in ceramics

LEAD (PbO) has been mentioned frequently before as one of the major low-fire fluxes. There are several reasons for its popularity. It combines readily with all other fluxes and has a lower coefficient of expansion than the alkaline fluxes. Lead gives a greater brilliancy to the glaze, though at times this may be a disadvantage. The lead glazes melt and flow well and thus tend to reduce pinholes and other defects of the more viscous-type glazes. The chief defects are the poisonous nature of lead compounds unless they are fritted, and its weakness to attack by strong fruit acids. Lead tends to blacken or film over if slightly reduced. The surface of lead glazes tends to scratch easily unless used in conjunction with an alkaline flux. There are many forms of lead such as:

Galena (PbS)

Litharge (PbO)

Red lead (Pb_3O_4)

White lead [$2PbCO_3 \cdot Pb(OH_2)$]

Lead monosilicate, the fritted lead silicate composed of approximately 16 percent SiO_2 and 84 percent PbO.

Lead bisilicate, another commercial lead silicate having the approximate composition of 65 percent PbO, 33 percent SiO_2, and 2 percent Al_2O_3.

Sources of Neutral (R₂O₃) Oxides

Unlike the RO group which has numerous somewhat similar compounds, the R_2O_3 group is almost limited to alumina (Al_2O_3) or a few oxides which have the same oxygen ratio. The greatest difference between a glass and a glaze is the presence of alumina. The alumina content is a most important factor in a successful glaze. It controls the fluidity of the melting glaze and enables it to withstand the temperatures needed to mature the body. Greater amounts of alumina increase the hardness of the glaze and its resistance to abrasions and acids.

ALUMINA (Al_2O_3) in a glaze may vary from 0.1 to 0.9 molecular equivalents, depending upon firing temperatures. The equivalent ratios between the alumina and the silica groups may be from 1:4 to 1:20. For glossy glazes the ratio is about 1:10. As mentioned before, an increase of alumina will tend to bring about mat textures. A glossy porcelain glaze firing from cones 10 to 12 will have an alumina-silica ratio of between 1:7 and 1:8 whereas the mats will be 1:3.2 to 1:3.8. Alumina also has an effect on the colors developed. The normal blue of cobalt oxide will become a rose pink in the absence of alumina. Chromium oxide which usually gives various green tones will tend to become reddish in the presence of excess alumina. Sources of alumina are:

Alumina hydrate [$Al(OH)_3$]
Feldspars and Cornwall Stone (see sections under RO oxides)
Kaolin (china clay) $Al_2O_3 \cdot 2SiO_2 \cdot 2H_2O$ (see sections under Clay)

BORON (B_2O_3) is one of the neutral oxides (R_2O_3), which, by our previous definition, can react either as bases or acids. The refractory properties of alumina are more like those of the acid, silica, than any of the bases. Boric oxide has a number of characteristics similar to alumina: the alumina of mat glazes can be satisfactorily replaced by boric oxide, color effects do not change by this substitution, both alumina and boric oxide harm under-glaze red and green colors, and both can form mixed crystals.

On the whole, however, boric oxide functions as a base since in comparison with silica it increases the elasticity, lowers the tensile strength, and in limited quantities lowers the thermal coefficient of expansion. Like lead, it increases the gloss or refractive index of the glaze. Major compounds containing boron are:

Boric acid ($B_2O_3 \cdot 2H_2O$)
Borax ($Na_2 \cdot 2B_2O_3 \cdot 10H_2O$)
Colemanite ($2CaO \cdot 3B_2O_3 \cdot 5H_2O$), technically called calcium borate

ANTIMONY (Sb$_2$O$_3$) oxide is primarily used as an opacifier and a coloring agent and is found in:

Antimonious oxide (Sb$_2$O$_3$)

Basic antimonate of lead, [Pb$_3$(SbO$_4$)$_2$], also known as Naples yellow.

CHROMIUM or CHROMIC OXIDE (Cr$_2$O$_3$) is derived from the mineral chromite (FeCr$_2$O$_4$). It is used as a colorant in glazes. The fact that the mineral form is a natural spinel would indicate its use as a stain.

RED or FERRIC IRON OXIDE (Fe$_2$O$_3$) is commonly used as a coloring agent to form brownish red hues and also to modify copper and cobalt. It would have use as a flux were it not for its strong coloring action. Its presence in many compounds is regarded as an impurity and considerable effort goes into removing iron flecks from whiteware bodies. It conforms to the R$_2$O$_3$ oxide ratio but has none of the refractory qualities that alumina has.

Sources of Acid (RO$_2$) Oxides

The important oxide in this group, silica, has a refractory effect on the glaze while the others function largely as opacifiers or coloring agents.

SILICA (SiO$_2$) combines readily with the bases to form glassy silicates. It is the most common element in the glaze, comprising about 50 percent of it by weight. In a glaze it has the effect of raising the melting point, decreasing its fluidity, increasing resistance of the glaze to water and chemicals, increasing hardness and tensile strength, and reducing the coefficients of thermal expansion of the glaze. The amounts of silica used depend upon the flux and the maturing point of the glaze, but it is generally between 1 and 6 molecular equivalents.

Silica (SiO$_2$) is commonly obtained from sandstone, quartz sands, or flint pebbles. Silica is found combined with many ceramic materials which have been mentioned before. Below are listed a few of the more frequently used silica compounds.

Ball clay (Al$_2$O$_3$·2SiO$_2$·2H$_2$O)

Kaolin (Al$_2$O$_3$·2SiO$_2$·2H$_2$O)

Soda feldspar (Na$_2$O·Al$_2$O$_3$·6SiO$_2$)

Potash feldspar (K$_2$O·Al$_2$O$_3$·6SiO$_2$)

Cornwall stone (1RO·2.5Al$_2$O$_3$·20SiO$_2$)

Lepidolite (LiF·KF·Al$_2$O$_3$·3SiO$_2$)

Spodumene (Li$_2$O·Al$_2$O$_3$·4SiO$_2$)

TIN (SnO_2) is used primarily as an opacifier in glazes. Although rather expensive it has a continued wide use because it has greater covering power than any other opacifier.

Tin oxide (SnO_2), also called *stannic oxide*, is the chief form of tin used.

TITANIUM (TiO_2) is probably the only other oxide in the RO_2 group which has some of the refractory qualities of silicon. Its use in glazes, however, is entirely due to its effect upon other colors and as an opacifier.

Titanium dioxide (TiO_2)

Rutile (TiO_2), an impure form containing iron oxide.

Characteristics of Ceramic Chemicals

ALBANY SLIP is a slip clay, which is a natural clay containing silica, alumina, and fluxes in the correct proportions to function as a glaze. It is mined in the vicinity of Albany, New York, hence its name. Since it occurs in small pits, its composition and color will vary. Usually it fires a glossy brown-black at temperatures between cones 8 to 12. One shipment that I used, however, fired out a pale, nearly transparent tan. Slip clays are usually very easy to apply and fire with little, if any, defects. A typical composition and formula is as follows:

Composition

Silica	56.75%	Magnesia	3.23%
Alumina	15.47	Titania	1.00
Ferric oxide	5.73	Alkalies	3.25
Lime	5.78		

Formula

0.195 K_2O	0.608 Al_2O_3	3.965 SiO_2
0.459 CaO	0.081 Fe_2O_3	
0.345 MgO		

ALUMINA HYDRATE [$Al(OH)_3$] is preferred to the calcined form (Al_2O_3) for some uses since it has better adhesive qualities and stays suspended in the glaze longer. Introduction of alumina for mat effects is considered to be more effective in the hydrate form than in such compounds as clay or feldspar.

ANTIMONIOUS OXIDE (Sb_2O_3) is poisonous and slightly soluble in water. For satisfactory effect as an opacifier it must be used in glazes firing under cone 1. Antimony is also used to produce yellow and orange colors for glazes. The most common mixture is known as *yellow base* and has the following composition:

Red lead	15
Antimony oxide	10
Tin oxide	4

The mixture is calcined to cone 09, then ground and washed.

BASIC ANTIMONATE of LEAD [$Pb_3(SbO_4)_2$], also known as *Naples yellow*, is primarily used as a paint pigment. It is a source of low-fire yellows. The presence of lead in Naples yellow is an advantage since antimony will not produce a yellow unless combined with lead or iron.

BARIUM CARBONATE (Ba_2CO_3) is usually used in combination with other fluxes since at lower temperatures it combines very slowly and reacts as a refractory to form mat textures. At higher temperatures it reacts strongly as a flux.

BARIUM CHROMATE ($BaCrO_4$) is used to produce colors in the pale-yellow to light-green range. It is generally used in overglaze decoration as it is fugitive at temperatures over cone 04.

BENTONITE ($Al_2O_3 \cdot 4SiO_2 \cdot 9H_2O$) is derived from volcanic ash. This formula is not quite correct as bentonite contains other impurities. South Dakota bentonite has the following analysis:

Silica	64.23%	Lime	0.46%
Alumina	20.74	Magnesia	2.26
Iron oxide	3.49		

It generally fires to a light cream and fuses at about 2400°F. Its chief value is its use as a plasticizer for short clays. As such it is about five times as effective as ball clay. Purified bentonite will also make a stronger glaze covering and will help prevent settling in the glaze. An addition of about 3 percent is sufficient.

BICARBONATE OF SODA ($NaHCO_3$) has some use in casting slips and in forming stains with cobalt sulfate. Soda ash (Na_2CO_3) is the sodium form more commonly used as a flux.

BISMUTH SUBNITRATE ($BiONO_3 \cdot H_2O$) generally contains impurities such as arsenic, lead, and silver carbonates. It melts at a low temperature and is used primarily to produce pearly metallic lusters under reducing conditions. (See Luster Glazes).

BONE ASH in the unrefined state has a formula of $4Ca_3(PO_4)_2 \cdot CaCO_3$ with a molecular weight of 1340. The material generally used today is the refined calcium phosphate $Ca_3(PO_4)_2$ with a molecular weight of 310. It is sometimes used as a glaze flux but more commonly as a body ingredient in bone china, chiefly that produced in England. It lowers the firing temperatures required and increases the translucency.

BORAX ($Na_2O \cdot 2B_2O_3 \cdot 10H_2O$) is, next to lead, the major low-fired flux. It has a strong action on all ceramic compounds and may be even used in small amounts in the higher-fired glazes which tend to be overly viscous in nature. Borax has a different effect upon coloring oxides than lead and for this reason it is often used either alone or in combination with lead. Borax absorbs moisture and should therefore be kept dry or weight calculations will be inaccurate. As mentioned earlier, borax is very soluble in water and should not be used on raw ware.

BORIC ACID ($B_2O_3 \cdot 2H_2O$) is a flaky material soluble in water. It is available in a fairly pure state at a low price. Although boron is one of the neutral oxides (R_2O_3), it functions more as a base since it increases the gloss like lead. Unlike silica, an acid, boron lowers the expansion coefficient and increases the elasticity.

CADMIUM SULFIDE (CdS) is a low-fire yellow colorant. It is usually combined in a stain made of cadmium, selenium, and sulphur frits. Unfortunately it is fugitive above cone 010 and can only be used for overglaze decorations.

CALCIUM BORATE (See Colemanite).

CALCIUM CARBONATE (See Whiting).

CALCIUM FLUORIDE (See Fluorspar).

CALCIUM PHOSPHATE (See Bone Ash).

CALCIUM ZIRCONIUM SILICATE is a commercially produced opacifier with the composition of ZrO_2, 51.12 percent; SiO_2, 25.41 percent; CaO, 22.23 percent. It does not have the strength of tin but is considerably cheaper. It will lower slightly the maturing temperatures of the lower-fired glazes.

CAROLINA STONE is similar to Cornwall stone. See Page 137.

CHINA CLAY (See Kaolin).

CHROMIUM OXIDE (Cr_2O_3) and other chromium compounds are commonly used in glazes to produce green colors. Dichromates are preferred because of the greater amounts of chromium per weight. Care must be taken in the glaze composition for, when combined with tin, a pink will result. Zinc will form a brown and high-lead glazes may develop a yellow-lead chromate. Reducing conditions in the kiln will blacken the color. In fact even adjacent tin-glazed and chrome-glazed pieces may affect each other in the kiln. Bright low-temperature reds (under cone 010) may be produced by chrome oxide in a high-lead and low-alumina glaze.

CLAY (See Chapter 1, "Clay") is a decomposed feldspathic-type rock consisting chiefly of silicates of aluminum but often containing numerous other ingredients such as quartz, micas, feldspars, iron oxides, carbonates of calcium and magnesium, and organic matter.

COBALT CARBONATE ($CoCO_3$) is used to introduce a blue glaze color, and in combinations with manganese, iron chromate, or ochre to produce black colorants.

COBALT OXIDE (Co_2O_3) is the major blue colorant. It is extremely strong and therefore often fritted with alumina and lime or with lead for lower-fired underglaze colors. The frit allows a lighter and more an even color dispersion. Color stains made of cobalt, alumina, and zinc are uniform at all temperature ranges. Small amounts of cobalt in combination with MgO, SiO_2, and B_2O_3 will produce a variety of hues in the pink and lavender range.

COBALT SULFATE ($CoSo_4 \cdot 7H_2O$), unlike the other cobalt compounds mentioned, is very soluble in water. It melts at a low temperature and is primarily used in decorative work or lusterware.

COLEMANITE ($2CaO \cdot 3B_2O_3 \cdot 5H_2O$) is a natural hydrated calcium borate, which has the advantage of being only slightly soluble in water and therefore does not develop the granular lumps in the glaze so characteristic of borax. Colemanite has wide use as a low-fire flux since the boron present melts at a fairly low temperature. It tends to prevent crazing and also functions slightly as an opacifier. Colemanite may be substituted for calcium in some glazes where its presence would harm pink or red colors desired. Colemanite may vary slightly in composition depending upon its source and this factor may cause trouble until tests are made.

COPPER CARBONATE ($CuCO_3$) is a major green colorant used in glazes. The carbonate form is preferred to the oxide form in the production of blue greens or copper reds under reducing conditions.

COPPER OXIDE is (1) cupric or black copper oxide (CuO) or (2) cuprous or red copper oxide (Cu_2O). Copper is one of the few colorants which does not change greatly under normal oxidizing conditions. Lead fluxes tend to produce a blackish green. When copper and tin are used with an alkaline flux, a turquoise will result. Potash will induce a yellowish green while zinc and copper with fluxes of sodium, potassium, and barium will tend to develop a blue tinge.

CORNWALL STONE is a complex mixture derived from an English deposit of partially decomposed granite rock. It is composed of quartz (flint), feldspar, lepidolite, tourmaline, fluorspar, and small quantities of other minerals. Cornwall stone has characteristics which lie between those of kaolin and feldspar. It is a major ingredient of many English glazes and bodies and is subject to less firing strains than is a body composed of kaolin and feldspar. Due to the more intimate mixture of naturally occurring minerals a smaller amount of alkali flux is necessary than would otherwise be needed. Since less bulk is required there is less shrinkage of both the unfired and fired glaze, thus minimizing glaze defects. Cornwall stone is roughly similar to *petuntze*, the feldspathic powered rock used for centuries by the Chinese as a major ingredient in their porcelain bodies and glazes. An average analysis of 12 Cornwall stone samples gives the following ceramic formula:

0.63 KNaO   1.3497 Al$_2$O$_3$ 10.1227 SiO$_2$
0.32 CaO   0.0181 Fe$_2$O$_3$ 0.785 H$_2$O
0.05 MnO

The very similar material is mined in the United States under the name of *Carolina stone*. It can, with slight additions, be substituted for Cornwall stone. A comparison between two samples is as follows:

	Cornwall stone	Carolina stone
SiO$_2$	71.10%	72.30%
Al$_2$O$_3$	16.82	16.23
Fe$_2$O$_3$	0.16	0.07
CaO	1.60	0.62
MgO	0.05	trace
K$_2$O	6.57	4.42
Na$_2$O	2.29	4.14
CaF$_2$	0.50	1.23
Ignition loss	1.25	1.06

CRYOLITE (Na$_3$AlF$_6$) is used primarily as a flux and an opacifier for enamels and glasses. It has a limited use in glazes and bodies as a source of fluxes and alumina. In some glazes an addition of cryolite will promote crazing.

DOLOMITE [CaMg (CO$_3$)$_2$] is a double carbonate of calcia and magnesia. It has a greater use in glassmaking than in glazes. It is a cheap method of introducing calcia and magnesia into a glaze. Dolomite will promote a longer and lower firing range in clay bodies. Below cone 4 the addition of a small amount of a lower-firing alkaline flux to the dolomite will greatly increase this effect.

EPSOM SALTS (See Magnesium Sulfate).

FELDSPAR is a crystalline rock composed of the aluminum silicates of potassium, sodium, and calcium. These silicates are never found in a pure state but in a mixture with one or the other predominating. For convenience in ceramic calculations their formulas are usually given as follows:

Potash feldspar (microcline)
  K$_2$O·Al$_2$O$_3$·6SiO$_2$
Soda feldspar (albite) Na$_2$O·Al$_2$O$_3$·6SiO$_2$
Lime feldspar (anorthite) CaO·Al$_2$O$_3$·6SiO$_2$

The feldspars are a major ingredient of porcelain and whiteware bodies and are often the only source of body flux. If the feldspar content of the body is high, the substitution of a potash feldspar by soda spar will reduce the vitrification point by as much as 100°F. The feldspars are a cheap source of glaze flux and have the additional advantage of being nonsoluble. Due to the presence of Al$_2$O$_3$ and SiO$_2$ the feldspar cannot be considered a flux at low temperature ranges even though some flux is contributed to the glaze. The fluxing action is increased by the fineness of the particle size. Potash forms a harder glaze than soda and decreases the thermal expansion. Thus, unless soda is desired for color purposes, potash feldspar should be preferred in the glaze composition.

FERRIC CHLORIDE (FeCl$_3$·6H$_2$O) is more commonly called *chloride of iron*. It is very soluble in water and must be stored in airtight containers. Its chief use is as a lustre decoration on glass or glazes. It produces a irridescent gold-colored film under proper conditions. (See Lustre Glazes.)

FERRIC OXIDE (See Iron Oxide).

FERROUS OXIDE (See Iron Oxide).

FLINT (SiO$_2$) is also called silica or, in foreign publications, quartz. It is commonly obtained from sandstone, quartz sands, or flint pebbles. True flint is obtained from England, France, and Denmark, and is prepared by calcining and grinding flint beach pebbles. This cryptocrystalline has a different specific gravity (2.33) from that prepared from quartz sand or sandstone (2.65). In the United States, all silica is called *flint*. The difference between the two is slight. The "pebble" flint reacts a trifle faster in the glaze. The specific gravity is of importance only if it is used in casting slips.

When used alone silica melts at the extremely high temperature of 3119°F. It forms an extremely hard and stable crystal. It combines under heat, however, with a variety of fluxes at much lower temperatures to form a glass and with the alumina compounds to form the more refractory body structure. An increase in the silica content of a glaze has the effect of raising the maturing temperatures as well as increasing its hardness and resistance to wear. In a glaze the addition of flint decreases its thermal expansions but in a body it increases such expansions.

FLUORSPAR (CaF_2), also called *calcium fluoride*, has a limited use as a source of flux in glaze and body compositions. The particle size must be under 100 mesh when used in the body or pinholes are likely to form in the glaze. Fluorspar fluxes at a lower temperature than other calcia compounds. With copper oxides some unusual blue-green hues can be developed.

ILMENITE ($TiO_2 \cdot FeO$) is the mineral source of titanium and its compounds. Used as a coarse powderlike sand it produces dark specks in the glaze.

IRON CHROMATE ($FeCrO_4$) is used in combination with manganese and zinc oxide to produce underglaze brown colors or with cobalt to form a black stain. Used alone it is fugitive above cone 04.

IRON OXIDES have three forms: (FeO) *ferrous oxide;* (Fe_2O_3) *ferric oxide*, hematite;

and (Fe_3O_4) *ferrous-ferric oxide*, magnetite. Iron is the oxide most frequently used to produce tan or brown bodies and glazes. Were it not for its pronounced color it would have a wide use as a flux. It is responsible for most of the low-firing characteristics and the red color of many earthenware clays. A pink stain can be made with a smaller amount of iron plus alumina, calcium, and flint. When reduced in a suitable glaze iron will form grey-greens. (See Celadon.)

KAOLIN ($Al_2O_3 \cdot 2SiO_2 \cdot 2H_2O$) is also called *china clay* or *pure clay*. Due to its composition and relative purity kaolin is the highest firing clay. It is an important ingredient of all whiteware and china bodies since it fires out pure white. For glazes kaolin constitutes a major source of Al_2O_3 and SiO_2. The chief residual deposits are in North Carolina and sedimentary deposits are found in South Carolina and Georgia. For bodies the more plastic sedimentary types are preferred. The sedimentary kaolin deposits of Florida are even more plastic and are often termed ball kaolin. (See Chapter 1, "Clay.")

LEAD ANTIMONATE (See Basic Antimonate of Lead).

LEAD, BISILICATE (See Lead Silicate).

LEAD, WHITE (See Lead Carbonate).

LEAD CARBONATE [$2PbCO_3 \cdot Pb(OH)_2$] is the white powder more commonly called white lead. It is the major low-fired flux and produces a glossy glaze with relatively few faults. Its major drawback is its poisonous effects if breathed in while carelessly sprayed. A lead-glazed vessel should not be used for storing concentrated citric acid fruit juices. By fritting the lead and silica this dust hazard and most of the solubility danger can be removed. But due to its ease of application and free flowing and brilliant surface, lead carbonate continues to be the major low-fired flux. The evolution of CO_2 from the glazes is said to promote a better mixture of the glaze ingredients than that of other lead compounds. The use of lead as a flux will have a different effect on the colorants used than the alkaline compounds. The addition of calcia, silica, or alumina to a lead glaze will increase its hardness and resistance to wear.

LEAD OXIDE as used in ceramics is of two types: *litharge* or lead monoxide (PbO) and *red lead* or minium (Pb_3O_4). Litharge is a yellow powder which has a greater use in Europe than in the United States. As litharge occasionally contains impurities and has larger particles than the carbonate form, the latter is the preferred lead compound to use. Due to the greater amount of oxygen the red form is often used in place of litharge. Ceramic grades of red lead are seldom pure but usually contain 75 percent red lead and about 25 percent litharge. Pound for pound red lead contains more PbO than the carbonate form.

LEAD SILICATE is a frit made of lead and silica to eliminate the toxic effects of the lead compounds. The two most common types are: *lead monosilicate*, with a composition of 15 percent SiO_2 and 85 percent PbO; *lead bisilicate*, with a formula of 65 percent PbO, 34 percent SiO_2, and 1 percent Al_2O_3.

LEAD SILICATE, HYDROUS [$2PbSiO_2 \cdot Pb(OH)_2$] has a molecular weight of 807. This material is the basic silicate of white lead. It is used as a substitute for lead carbonate when the CO_2 released by the carbonate forms pinholes or is otherwise objectionable in the glaze.

LEAD SULFIDE (PbS), also called *galena*, is the black powder which is the raw source of all lead compounds. It has a very limited use in glazes.

LEPIDOLITE ($LiF \cdot KF \cdot Al_2O_3 \cdot 3SiO_2$), also called lithium mica, contains from 3 to 6 percent of lithia. It has some use as a body ingredient in chinaware bodies as well as a source of flux, Al_2O_3, and SiO_2 in the higher-temperature glazes. It will tend to brighten most glazes, lower thermal expansions, and reduce brittleness. (See Lithium Carbonate.)

LIME (CaO), calcium oxide (See Whiting).

LITHARGE (PbO) (See Lead Oxide).

LITHIUM CARBONATE (Li_2CO_3) is a common source of lithia which is a strong flux in the higher temperature ranges. With lithia greater amounts of Al_2O_3, SiO_2, and CaO may be used in alkaline glazes, thus producing a more durable glaze, while retaining the unusual copper blues characteristic of the alkaline-type glazes. It may be used in place of lead in the medium temperature ranges when volitization is a problem.

MAGNESIUM CARBONATE ($MgCO_3$) magnesite acts as a refractory at lower temperatures, changing to a flux at higher temperatures. It is valuable to slow down to fluid qualities of crystalline and other runny glazes. It also improves glaze adherence.

MAGNESIUM SULFATE ($MgSO_4 \cdot 7H_2$) is better known as *epsom salts*. Its primary use in glazes is as an aid to retard the settling of frits and glazes. Usually 1 percent will be sufficient and will have no apparent effect on the glaze.

MAGNETITE (See Iron Oxides).

MANGANESE DIOXIDE (See Manganese Oxide).

MANGANESE OXIDE (MnO_2) is used in ceramics as a colorant. It should not be used in concentrations over 5 percent to either body or glaze or blisters may develop. The usual colors produced are in the brown range. With cobalt a black results and with the proper alkaline fluxes purple and dark reddish hues may develop. When fritted with alumina a pink colorant will be formed.

NEPHELINE SYENITE ($K_2O \cdot 3Na_2O \cdot 4Al_2O_3 \cdot 9SiO_2$) is a material roughly similar to a feldspar and has the following composition.

SiO_2	60.4 %	*Molecular formula*		
Al_2O_3	23.6	Na_2O	0.713	Al_2O_3 1.04
Fe_2O_3	0.08	K_2O	0.220	
CaO	0.7	CaO	0.056	SiO_2 4.53
MgO	.1	MgO	0.011	
Na_2O	9.8			
K_2O	4.7		*Molecular weight* 447	
Ignition				
loss	0.7			

A major use for nepheline syenite is as a substitute for potash feldspar where it lowers the firing temperatures required. It also produces a greater firing range and increased thermal expansion which in turn will reduce crazing tendencies in the glaze. Its use in a glaze is roughly similar to potash feldspar with the exception of the lower maturing point.

NICKEL OXIDE is used in two forms; (NiO) nickelous or *green nickel oxide*, and (Ni_2O_3) nickelic or *black nickel oxide*. The function of nickel in a glaze is almost solely as a colorant. Depending upon the flux used and ratio of alumina a variety of colors may be produced; with zinc, a blue is obtained; with lime, tan; with barium, brown, and with magnesia, green. None of these hues are particularly brilliant. In general nickel is used to soften and alter other coloring oxides. In addition, the use of 5 to 10 percent nickel in a proper glaze results in the formation of a crystalline structure.

OCHRE is a term given to clays containing varying amounts of red iron or manganese oxides. Their chief use is in paint manufacturing. However, they may be used as glaze or slip colorants to impart tan, brown or brick-red hues.

OPAX is a standard commercially produced opacifier with the following composition:

ZrO_2	91.88%	$NaKO$	.92%
TiO_2	.40	Al_2O_3, P_2O_5	.39
LiO_2	5.76	Total H_2O	.09
Fe_2O_3	.06		

Opax does not have the power of tin oxide, but it is considerably cheaper and is often used to replace part of the tin oxide which would otherwise be required.

PEARL ASH (See Potassium Carbonate).

PETALITE ($Li_2O \cdot Al_2O_3 \cdot SiO_2$) is a source of lithia and silica for medium- and high-temperature glazes. It tends to lower the maturing temperature ranges and to lessen thermal expansions when used in either a body or glaze.

POTASH FELDSPAR (See Feldspar).

POTASSIUM CARBONATE (K_2CO_3) is more commonly called *pearl ash*. It is used primarily to modify color effects. When pearl ash is substituted for the lead, sodium, or calcium content, the colors resulting from copper oxide may be changed from the usual green to either a yellow green or a bright blue.

POTASSIUM DICHROMATE ($K_2Cr_2O_7$) is used in glazes as a green colorant. When it is calcined with tin, low-fire stains developing pink and red hues are formed. (See Chromium Oxide.)

PYROPHYLLITE ($Al_2O_3 \cdot 4SiO_2 \cdot H_2O$) is used primarily in wall-tile bodies where it decreases thermal expansions, crazing, and moisture expansions to which tile is subjected. Since it is nonplastic, it has a limited use in pottery bodies.

RED LEAD (See Lead Oxide).

SELENIUM (Se) has its greatest use as a glass colorant. It has a limited use in ceramic glazes and overglaze colors, primarily as cadmium-selenium red frits. These, unfortunately, are fugitive at higher temperatures.

SILICA (See Flint).

SILICON CARBIDE (SiC) has many industrial uses. Its value in ceramics is as sole or major ingredient in high-temperature kiln furniture and muffles. When added to an alkaline glaze in small amounts ($\frac{1}{2}$ of 1 percent), the carbon will reduce locally the copper oxides to form artificial copper reds.

SILVER CHLORIDE (AgCl) is the major silver compound used in luster overglaze preparations (See Lusters). When silver chloride is combined with bismuth and with a resin or fat oil as a binder, an overglaze metallic luster with a greenish or yellow tints will form. Silver chloride must be fired in a low temperature reducing atmosphere.

SODA ASH (See Sodium Carbonate).

SODIUM ALUMINATE ($Na_2O \cdot Al_2O_3$) is used to prevent casting slips from setting and to increase the strength of dry ware.

SODIUM BICARBONATE (See Bicarbonate of Soda).

SODIUM CARBONATE (Na_2CO_3) is commonly called *soda ash*. It is a very active flux but because of its solubility it is more commonly used in glazes as a frit ingredient. Small quantities of soda ash will reduce the water of plasticity required in a clay body, thus increasing its workability and strength

and reducing the shirnkage when it goes from the wet to the dry state.

SODIUM SILICATE ($Na_2 \cdot XSiO_2$) is a compound which may vary from $1Na_2O \cdot 1.6SiO_2$ to $1Na_2O \cdot 3.75SiO_2$. It usually comes in a liquid form and is the major defofocculant used in casting slips. Like soda ash it greatly reduces the water required to make the clay into a slip form. In doing so it greatly lessens the rates of shrinkage, the strains of drying, and breakage in the green and dry states.

SODIUM URANATE ($Na_2O \cdot UO_3$), more commonly called *uranium yellow* has unfortunately not been available since World War II because of restrictions placed on uranium by the Atomic Energy Commission. Uranium yellows are still available, however, in Europe. Uranium compounds were formerly the best source of yellow colorants. When uranium compounds are combined with various fluxes, or with tin and zirconium oxide, a variety of hues from bright yellow to orange, to vermillion red can be developed. The only uranium compounds now available to the potter are depleted ores which are highly radioactive and dangerous under the conditions in which the average studio potter must work.

SPODUMENE ($Li_2O \cdot Al_2O_3 \cdot 4SiO_2$) is an important source of lithia. The use of lithia, which is an active flux, helps to develop unusual copper-blue hues. Spodumene is also used in whiteware and porcelain bodies. When used to replace feldspar it will reduce the vitrification temperature as well as the shrinkage rate. Strange as it may seem, the crystalline form of spodumene expands at about 1700°F instead of shrinking. When a mixture of 60-percent spodumene and 40-percent lead bisilicate is used, a nonplastic, press-formed body can be made which, at 1970°F, will have zero absorption and zero shrinkage.

STEATITE (See Talc), a hydrous magnesium silicate, is a massive variety of talc. Most steatite is used in a powdered form for electrical insulators. It has very little shrinkage and occasionally the rocklike nuggets are turned down in a lathe for special projects. Steatite was used by the Egyptians some 5000 years ago for beads and small figurines. These were generally covered by a turquoise alkaline copper glaze.

TALC varies from $3MgO \cdot 4SiO_2 \cdot H_2O$ to $4MgO \cdot 5SiO_2 \cdot H_2O$. In the solid and more impure form it is also known as *steatite* and *soapstone*. Talc is occasionally used in glazes but is more frequently employed as a major ingredient in whiteware bodies firing at moderate temperatures (cones 04-6). Like dolomite, it is used to lower the firing temperatures of the kaolin, ball clays, and feldspars which are often the other body ingredients.

TIN OXIDE (SnO_2), also called *stannic oxide*, is the most effective of all opacifiers. From 5 to 7 percent will produce a completely opaque white glaze. An excess will produce a dull surface. Tin also has a wide use in stains as it has a considerable effect on the color qualities of most color-forming oxides. Due to its relatively high price tin substitutes are frequently used. (See Opacifiers.)

TITANIUM OXIDE (TiO_2), or more correctly *titanium dioxide*, is a major opacifier when used either alone or in a frit. Like rutile, which is an impure form containing iron, titanium will, if used in any quantity, encourage a semimat surface texture.

URANIUM OXIDE (see Sodium Uranate).

VANADIUM PENTOXIDE (V_2O_5) is a rather weak yellow colorant when used alone. When fritted in the proper composition with tin, it produces a strong yellow color. This stain, known commercially as tin-vanadium stain, has largely replaced the uranium yellows which are no longer available. It has a wide firing range (cones 06-14), is transparent, and is not affected by a reduction firing.

VOLCANIC ASH occurs in many regions of the American West. It was formed from the dust of volcanic glass erupted in prehistoric volcanic actions. Since the material often floated through the air many miles before being deposited, it is extremely fine and can be used with little preparation. Its composition is roughly similar to that of a granite-type rock (see the formula under RO oxides). An average analysis of Kansas ash is as follows:

SiO_2	72.51%	MgO	0.07%
Al_2O_3	11.55	K_2O	7.87
Fe_2O_3	1.21	Na_2O	1.79
TiO_2	0.54	Ignition loss	3.81
CaO	0.68		

In most glazes volcanic ash can be substituted for roughly 70 parts of feldspar and 30 parts of flint. A low-fired 04 glaze may be compounded of 60-percent ash and 40-percent borax and/or lead.

WHITING ($CaCO_3$) is a *calcium carbonate*, produced domestically by processing marble or limestone. European whiting is generally obtained from chalk deposits such as the famous cliffs of Dover. Whiting is the major high-fire flux although it has a minor use in bodies where a small amount will lower vitrification temperatures and reduce porosity. As a flux it produces much harder and tougher silicates than will either the lead or alkaline compounds. For this reason small amounts are often added to the lower-fired glazes. As with other fluxes calcium has an effect upon the coloring oxides, particularly chrome greens.

ZINC OXIDE (ZnO) is a strange compound

to classify. At high temperatures it is an active flux. When used to excess in a glaze high in alumina and cooled slowly, zinc will produce crystalline structures. Opacity will develop if zinc is used in a high-alumina low-calcium glaze with no borosilicate fluxes. In general zinc increases the maturing range and promotes a higher gloss, brighter colors, a reduction of expansions, and, under some conditions, an opacity.

ZIRCONIUM OXIDE (ZrO_2) is seldom used alone as an opacifier in ceramics but is generally combined with other oxides and fritted into a more stable silicate form. Below are listed a few commercial zirconium silicates. None have the strength of tin oxide but they are considerably cheaper.

Calcium zirconium silicate: 51.12% ZrO_2, 25.41% SiO_2, and 22.23% CaO.
Magnesium zirconium silicate: 53.75% ZrO_2, 29.92% SiO_2, and 18.54% MgO.
Zinc zirconium silicate: 45.78% ZrO_2, 23.08% SiO_2, and 30.52% ZnO.
Zirconium spinel: 39.94% ZrO_2, 25.25% SiO_2, 19.47% ZrO, and 19.41% Al_2O_3.

Most of the above compounds are used in combinations with other opacifiers such as tin or the titanium compounds. (See also Opax and Zircopax.)

ZIRCOPAX is a standard commercially produced opacifier with the composition of ZrO_2, 64.88 percent; TiO_2, 0.22 percent; SiO_2, 34.28 percent.

Colorants for Glazes and Decoration

COLORING OXIDES. In general, most studio potters obtain their glaze colors from the oxides or carbonates of the more common metals such as iron, copper, nickel, tin, zinc, and manganese. Other oxides, such as vanadium and cobalt, although rarer and more expensive, are extensively used because of a lack of cheaper substitutes. These compounds have been discussed in previous sections. The following list of major colors indicates the oxide necessary and the amounts generally used to produce the particular color. But just because an oxide is listed as producing a green does not mean that it will produce a green in every case. A study of the section on ceramic materials will reveal that generally the particular color which develops from an oxide depends upon the type of flux used, the proportions of alumina or silica, and the firing temperature. In some cases, even the rate of cooling will have an effect upon the glaze. Therefore, the list of oxides and colors on page 144 is merely for your convenience in determining color possibilities. Before using the oxide, look up its characteristics and that of the glaze in which you plan to use it.

As mentioned before, variations of the above colors will occur depending upon glaze compositions. It is common practice to use two or more colorants in order to modify harsh colors and to obtain subtle variations or mottled color effects. Copper and nickel are often used to soften powerful cobalt hues. Opacifiers are used to brighten colors. Rutile is a frequent

GUIDE TO USE OF COLORANTS

Color	Oxide	Percentage	Temperature	Atmosphere
BLACK				
	⎰cobalt	1–2	any	either
	⎱manganese	2–4		
	⎰cobalt	1		
	⎨iron	8	any	either
	⎱manganese	3		
BLUE				
	cobalt	½–1	any	either
	turquoise copper (alkaline flux)	3–5	low	oxidizing
	slate blue nickel (with zinc)	1–3	low	oxidizing
BROWN				
	rutile	5	any	reducing
	chromium (with MgO, ZnO)	2–5	low	either
	iron	3–7	any	oxidizing
	manganese	5	any	either
	nickel (with zinc)	2–4	any	either
GREEN				
	copper oxide	1–5	any	oxidizing
	iron	1–4	any	reducing
	nickel	3–5	low	oxidizing
RED				
	pink chrome-tin (1 to 18)	5	any	oxidizing
	coral chromium (with high PbO)	5	low	oxidizing
	purple manganese (with KNaO)	4–6	any	oxidizing
	copper	1	any	reducing
	iron (high SiO_2 = KNaO) no CaO	2–5	low	oxidizing
TAN				
	iron	2	any	either
	manganese	2	any	either
	rutile	2	any	either
YELLOW				
	uranium	5–10	any	oxidizing
	tin-vanadium stain	3–6	any	either

addition since it contributes a runny and slightly specked quality in addition to slightly matting a glaze.

OPACIFIERS are, for the most part, a group of chemicals which are relatively insoluble in the glaze melt. Tin oxide and zirconium oxide are the chief examples of this type. As such they remain suspended in the glaze and if dense enough prevent the light from penetrating through to the body. Most opacifiers, and of course those of the greatest value, are white. However, some give a slight yellow, pink, or bluish cast to the glaze.

Another type of opacifier is titanium (or zinc under some conditions) which tends to form minute crystalline structures within the glaze, having a different index of refraction from the major portion of the glaze, thus breaking up and preventing much of the light penetration. This is the type of crystal formation associated with mat glazes and is the reason why all mats must be, necessarily, either wholly or partially opaque.

OPACIFIERS

Color	Oxide	Percentage	Temperature	Atmosphere
Pure White	tin	5	any	either
Weak Blue White	titanium	8–12	any	either
White	zirconium	8–12	any	either
Weak Yellow White	antimony	10–12	low	oxidizing
Weak White	zinc	5	low	either
White	opax(a frit)	10	any	either
White	zircopax (a frit)	10	any	either

SPINEL STAINS. Under certain circumstances, the use of the raw coloring oxide may be objectionable. For example, most metallic oxides are very soluble in the melting glaze. In the previous section, we noted that the fluxes and other elements of the glaze had a considerable effect upon the color quality. Overglaze and underglaze decoration with any degree of precision or control is impossible with colorants which diffuse into or flow with the glaze. In these cases, a special type of colorant known as a spinel is used.

A spinel stain is a colored crystal that is extremely resistant to the attacks of fluxes in the glaze and the effects of high temperatures. In strict chemical terms, the term refers to the mineral magnesium aluminate ($MgAl_2O_3$). However, manganese, iron, and chromium may be present by replacement. The crystal is an octahedron variety of extreme hardness. The ruby gem is a red spinel. By calcining certain oxides together, some very stable colored spinels can be formed. In general, these follow the formula $RO:R_2O_3$. The RO member may be either MgO, ZnO, NiO, CaO, CdO, MnO, or FeO, and the R_2O_3 can be Cr_2O_3, Al_2O_3, or Fe_2O_3.

Preparation of a spinel stain is a lengthy procedure and it is not recommended unless it is necessary for advanced experimental work. There is a wide range of commercial stains, expertly prepared, available at a reasonable cost. The general idea, however, of the preparation should be understood. More detailed information can be found in the reference texts listed in the Appendix.

It is extremely necessary that the chemicals involved are mixed completely and intimately. To this end the raw chemicals should first be passed through an 80-mesh sieve. It is preferable that they be in the form of soluble salts, that is, the nitrates or sulfates of the oxides listed above. These are thoroughly mixed in a liquid solution. After the water has been evaporated, the dry mixture is placed in a crucible, or a kiln, and calcined. The temperature will vary with the mixture. If the mixture melts into a solid mass, the mixture should be calcined in a pot furnace so that the crucible can be removed with tongs and the contents poured into water, thus preventing the spinel from hardening into a solid crystalline block. Afterwards, the material is broken up with an iron mortar and pestle into a coarse powder which is then ball milled. For a uniform color without specks, the particle size of the spinel must be extremely small. This may necessitate grinding in the ball mill for well over a hundred hours. When it is ground fine enough, the stain should be washed several times with hot water to remove any remaining soluble salts. Filters may be necessary at this point to prevent the loss of fine particles.

OTHER COLORED STAINS. Besides the spinels, a number of other chemical compounds are calcined to produce stable colorants at certain temperatures. A discussion of a few of the better-known examples will serve to illustrate some of the numerous possibilities in the preparation of colorants.

An ultramarine blue can be formed by a silicate of cobalt. It is made by calcining cobalt oxide and flint plus a flux such as feldspar.

Green stains can be developed by calcining fluorspar and chromium oxide.

Yellow stains such as Naples yellow and yellow base are made from antimony, lead, and tin. Calcium and sodium uranate can also be used, when available, to form various yellow and orange colorants.

Pink and red stains are made by several methods. One of the most unusual is the precipitation of colloidal gold upon kaolin which is then calcined and ground to form the stain. Other red stains are formed from a mixture of tin, calcium, flint, and chromium. For further information and specific details consult the reference texts by Parmelee and Norton, and the "Literature Abstracts of Ceramic Glazes" listed in the Appendix.

UNDERGLAZE COLORS were briefly mentioned before in the section on decoration. As the term indicates, they are colors used under the glaze. Since they will eventually be fired at the same temperature as the glaze, the range of colors available is less than for overglaze colors. For example, at the hard porcelain range of cones 14 to 18, most, if not all, of the delicate hues available in overglaze colors will burn out completely. This leaves only the blues, browns, grays, gold pinks, reduction reds, and celadon hues available for use at these higher temperatures. It is advisable to run a series of firing tests before attempting any amount of decorative work at such temperatures. The basic reason for the use of underglaze rather than overglaze colors is one of durability. Its greatest use is in the field of dinnerware, especially restaurant china.

Underglaze colors are made up of a colorant, either a raw oxide or a spinel, a flux such as feldspar to allow the color to adhere to the body, and a dilutent like silica, calcined kaolin, or ground bisqueware. The purpose of these last materials is either to lighten the color or to equalize shrinkage. It is rather important that the mixture be adjusted properly to the bisque ware and the final glaze. The glazed surface should show no change in gloss over the decoration. A preliminary firing to red heat is necessary prior to glazing to burn out the vehicle used to adhere the mixture, which may be either a solution of gum tragacanth or oil of lavender thinned with turpentine. Failure to burn off the carbon formed by the adherent will make the glaze bubble and blister over the decoration.

OVERGLAZE COLORS. The major differences between overglaze colors and underglaze colors are the use of a lower melting flux and a wider range of colors. Since the decoration is to be applied to a completely glazed piece, the final firing need only be high enough to allow the flux to melt into the glaze and seal the color. This is usually at a temperature of cone 016, approximately 1460°F. The flux is made of varying proportions of lead, borax, and flint, depending upon the color to be used with it. The mixture is calcined lightly, ground, and washed. The colorant, and if necessary, an opacifier, is then added and the whole mixture ball milled to an adequate fineness. A vehicle such as gum or oil is used to help the mixture to adhere to the glazed surface. In commercial production where decoration is standardized and, a little sterile in design, printing methods are used. The colors of both types of decoration are applied by decals or silk screen.

LUSTERS. Since lusters are employed more as a decoration than as a glaze, they may be included in this section on decorative coloring materials. As was noted earlier in the discussion of glaze types, a luster is nothing more than a thin layer of metal which is deposited and fused upon the surface of the glaze. There are various methods by which this may be accomplished, some of which will be outlined below. Lusters may give a variety of effects depending upon the transparency or color of the composition and the type of glaze upon which it is applied. In the Persian and Hispano-Moresque pieces, it is usually very effectively combined with underglaze decoration. In fact, luster really comes into its own when it is used to enrich other types of decoration. If used alone in an over-all glaze effect, it tends to look like a rather cheap imitation of either glass or metal. The colors available in lusters are a transparent iridescent, a nacreous silver white, and metallic hues in a variety of yellows, greens, browns, and reds.

PREPARATION OF LUSTERS will vary according to the method of firing employed. In general they are of three types:

1. A mixture composed of a resin, oil of lavender, and a metallic salt is brushed on the glazed ware. The ware is then fired in an oxidizing kiln to a low temperature of between 1100° and 1300°F, at which point the carbon in the resin reduces the metallic salt to its metal form. Most lusters contain bismuth nitrate, an active flux, as well as the other metal salts. It is used in combination with zinc acetate, lead acetate, and alumina to produce a clear, iridescent luster. The various metal colorants are always used in the form of a salt which decomposes at the lower temperatures needed to form the luster coating. Yellows may be made with chrome alum and bismuth nitrate. Nickel nitrate, cobalt sulphate, manganese sulphate, and iron chloride will produce a variety of browns, shading from yellowish to red hues. Uranium nitrate, if ever again available, develops a greenish yellow. Gold is commonly used to produce red hues and platinum, silvery lusters. Many combinations of these colorants are used and results will be varied, depending in part upon the basic glaze used and the firing schedule. In general the luster mixture will consist of 1 part of the metallic salt, 3 to 5 parts resin, and 7 to 10 parts of oil of lavender. The resin, usually gum dammar, is heated; when it becomes liquid, the nitrate or chloride is added. When the nitrate dissolves, the oil is slowly poured in. The solution is then filtered, or cooled and decanted. Before creating your own formulas, read over the experiments listed in the "Literature Abstracts of Ceramic Glazes."

2. The method discussed above is the one which is commonly used today to produce lusters. Another type is similar to that used many centuries ago

by the Egyptian and Islamic potters. They first developed lusters and incidentally carried this decorative glaze to its highest level of artistic merit. The chief difference between the two methods is the use of a reduction fire to reduce the metal rather than the reducing agent contained in the resin. The mixture, which is brushed upon the glazed ware, consists of 3 parts metal, usually in a carbonate form, 7 parts red ochre, and an adhesive such as gum tragacanth. Old recipes call for vinegar or wine but the gum is doubtless more efficient. In the firing cycle, the atmosphere is oxidizing until a low red heat is reached, whereupon reduction is started and continued to the temperature necessary to reduce the metal, usually from 1200° to 1300°F.

3. The third method of developing a luster is also seldom used, but in rare cases it occurs by accident. The color is incorporated into the glaze, preferably in the form of a metallic salt. Various combinations may be used in proportions ranging from 0.5 to 8.0 percent of the total glaze. As in the resinate type of luster glaze, the use of bismuth in addition to the other metallic salts will aid luster development. The kiln is fired oxidizing to the maturity point of the glaze, then cooled to 1200° to 1300°F. At this point the kiln is relit and fired for about 15 minutes at a reducing atmosphere. Accurate records should be kept on reduction firings as variations of temperature and reduction periods will produce quite different results.

CHAPTER II

CERAMICS OF THE PAST

The history of ceramics begins with neolithic man. Pottery making doubtless began shortly after man was able to leave the nomadic life of the hunter,
at least for a portion of the year, for the more settled life of the herdsman,
fisherman, or seed-gatherer. Although estimates vary, it seems reasonable
to suppose that the first crude earthenware bowls were made not later than
8000 years ago. Dating from the same period or even earlier are the crude
figurines which served as fetishes or fertility symbols.

Since most societies venerated the dead, it was the custom, until recent
centuries, to place in the tomb the finest artifacts that the family of the
deceased could afford. Thus ceramic pieces, because of their durability,
have often provided us with the only account we have of many early
cultures. In this record can be traced the inventiveness and esthetic growth
of the human mind. The wanderings of man over the earth's surface, the
disasters of nature and war, and the intermingling of varied cultures have
also been recorded in fired clay.

In a single chapter it is impossible to give even a brief historical outline of
the field of the ceramics. Therefore, only the major ceramic periods will be
illustrated and their significant advances in design or technique will be
discussed briefly. An effort will be made to present pieces which are of
particular interest to the pottery student and to stress such areas as the
pre-Columbian which, unfortunately, are not featured in most museum
collections. In choosing to omit certain periods, I have been guided only
by my personal taste, or more correctly, prejudices. Little mention will
be made of eighteenth- and nineteenth-century European ware. This
period, that of the Industrial Revolution, produced several technical

Unglazed pottery jar with a thin slip decoration. Kansu, China, ca. 2000 B.C. Courtesy of The Metropolitan Museum of Art.

Pottery jar with double spiral design in slip. Kansu, China, 3000-2000 B.C. Courtesy of the Chicago Natural History Museum.

developments of commercial significance, but very little pottery of esthetic value.

Artistically, the average public and commercial taste is still not much more sophisticated than that of the Victorian Age. The "modern" façade of many articles produced today is unfortunately not so much the result of the acceptance of esthetic design concepts as the result of mass-production economies. This situation will prevail as long as values regarding art are held to be a matter of opinion rather than a matter of training and judgment.

Neolithic and Early Bronze-age Ceramics

No one culture invented pottery. Pottery making developed rather independently in various regions of the world when man learned to make fire and accidentally fired his first sun-dried clay pot. The prevalence of a basketlike texture design on many prehistoric pieces suggests that clay was first used to coat reed baskets, fitting them for the storage of wild-grain seeds. When one of these baskets was discarded and thrown on the fire, the greater hardness given the clay lining by the heat was noted. After this chance discovery had been observed, the first all-clay objects were made and fired. These early clay pots were impressed with a basketlike weave to resemble the reed baskets.

Whatever truth there is to this theory is unknown. Nevertheless, many

Predynastic pottery jar with a spiral decoration in thin slip. Egypt, before 3400 B.C. Courtesy of the Chicago Natural History Museum.

Banded unglazed earthenware vase, designed to suggest metal. China, Kansu, Shang Dynasty, 1766-1122 B.C. Courtesy of The Metropolitan Museum of Art.

early pottery fragments have this textured type of decoration. Pottery from this period has been found in such widespread locations as Egypt, South Russia, China, and both Americas. Besides impressed designs, another common early form of decoration was the spiral or double spiral. While the pieces illustrated are all unglazed earthenware, the kiln used must have been more advanced than the primitive kiln in order to prevent the slip designs from being discolored by haphazard reductions. Although hand-built, these neolithic pots display a feeling for form and appropriate decorations which were not far surpassed in the centuries that followed.

The beaker or vase from the Shang dynasty illustrated above (right) is interesting in that its foot rim and banded decoration are suggestive of a metal form. Throughout the history of the crafts there occur instances of such borrowing back and forth between media. In the long run these developments are apt to be detrimental since design is essentially a natural outgrowth of the possibilities inherent in a particular medium.

Pair of tomb horses with the dash and movement so characteristic of this period. China, Wei Dynasty, third century. Courtesy of The Art Institute of Chicago, Nickerson Collection.

Early Chinese Ceramic Sculpture

Illustrated in this section are several sculptural pieces dating from roughly 200 B.C. to A.D. 800 and covering the work of several important dynasties. This period was one of numerous invasions from the Tartars of the north. To such people the war horse was an important symbol and models of it were to be found in the tombs of all important personages. Buddhism was introduced from India in about A.D. 500. It was a vigorous and exciting age, perhaps not unlike that of Renaissance Italy (1300–1500), and no period of ceramic sculpture can compare with it. An amazing amount of ceramic sculpture was made—camels, horses, strange mythological beasts, guardian figures, comic pieces, portraits, and so forth. The horses are, of course, outstanding. Study the design of the horse's head shown on page 155. Equally powerful and yet sensitive were the portraits. Even such a mundane article as a candlestick was made with verve and imagination (see p. 155).

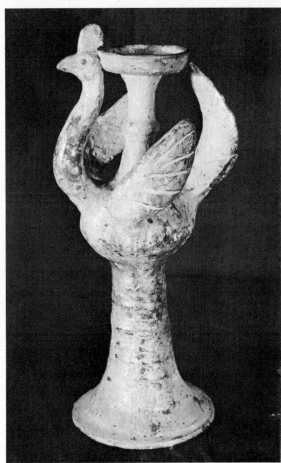

(Top, left) Strongly, modeled, hollow head of a tomb figure, slightly less than life size. China, T'ang Dynasty, 618-906. Courtesy of The Art Institute of Chicago, Gift of Mrs. C. Morse Ely. (Top, right) Pottery lampadere candlestick. China, Han Dynasty, 206 B.C.- A.D. 220. (Bottom) Model of a horse's head, tomb sculpture. China, Han Dynasty, 206 B.C.- A.D. 220. Courtesy of The Metropolitan Museum of Art.

(Left) Snake goddess, Crete, ca. 1575 B.C. (Right) Copy of the famous octopus bottle with a typical Minoan design. Crete, 1600-1500 B.C. Courtesy of The Metropolitan Museum of Art, Dodge Fund, 1914.

Mediterranean Pre-Greek Ware

The few examples of Mediterranean pre-Greek ware shown are from Etruscan and Cretan sources dating from 1600 to 500 B.C. A considerable amount of work was also done in Mesopotamia and in Egypt. Although all ceramics in this period were still made with earthenware bodies, glazes were in common use. The oldest positively dated glaze was found in Egypt on a green alkaline-glazed door tile from the tomb of King Menes (fl. 3400 B.C.). Glazes were also in use at an early date in Mesopotamia and India. There is some evidence to support the theory that glazes were introduced into China from the Middle East, but proof is not conclusive.

Pottery with a turned foot, indicating the use of a potter's wheel, has been found at a site in northern Iran and dated at about 4000 B.C. Use of the wheel spread rather slowly. By 1000 B.C. a considerable amount of pottery was still not wheel made. The reluctance of potters to use the wheel is understandable: The large storage jars then in common use could only be made by a thick-coil method and many smaller pieces were made in whole or part in a bisque clay mold.

Crete developed a rather advanced culture long before Greece, which eventually overpowered the island kingdom. The Cretan period, 3000 to 1500 B.C., is roughly comparable chronologically to the greatest period of Egyptian history. While Cretan sculpture and architecture did not compare with Egyptian work, their ceramics were far more varied and interesting. The bottle illustrated on this page is a fine example of the successful

(Left) Warrior Figure, terra cotta, 8 feet high. Modern copy in the Etruscan style. Courtesy of The Metropolitan Museum of Art. (Above) Etruscan oinochoë. Before 500 B.C. Courtesy of The Art Institute of Chicago, Gift of P. D. Armour and C. L. Hutchinson.

use of a realistic form as a design element. The little snake goddess shown on page 156 is also a delightfully fresh piece. While somewhat reminiscent of contemporary polychromed figurines, it nevertheless has a distinct quality and a forthright strength. Like the octopus bottle, it reflects the skillful use of a patterned design.

Little is known about the origin of the Etruscans. They were a seafaring people who came to central Italy in about the ninth century B.C. from an area in the Middle East near Syria. Their pottery was principally of the black type called *bucchero nero*. Much of it, unlike the vase shown on this page, had a raised or impressed design. When slip-decorated, the early ware was apt to feature flowers, horses, and so forth, showing a Persian influence. The most significant Etruscan work, however, was in the field of ceramic sculpture. The cornices and façades of their temples were covered with polychromed ware. An unusual but traditional ceramic piece was the burial coffin, often surmounted by a reclining figure, comfortably leaning on one elbow. Married couples were usually pictured together in the tomb statues, conversing, eating grapes, drinking. The warrior shown on this page is a contemporary Italian work of about 30 years ago reflecting the vigor of the Etruscan with a touch of Maillol; although a forgery, it is a most impressive piece of work. It is made of red clay and decorated with clay slips. The torso and upper part of the legs are hollow, and the arms, fired separately, were joined to the body by metal pins.

Storage jar in the famous dipylon style, geometric period, 39 inches high. Greece, eighth century B.C. Courtesy of The Metropolitan Museum of Art, Rogers Fund, 1914.

The Greek Period

The development of Greek ceramics follows the familiar pattern of the rise of a vigorous art form, the gradual solution of technical problems, and finally a decadence in which the pottery vessel served only as a surface for pictorial decoration. Nineteenth-century art critics and historians admired most Greek ceramics of the later period and regarded them as the highest achievements in ceramics. Each age finds it necessary to rewrite or reinterpret history. Thus, our generation has reversed the evaluations of the romantic age of Byron. As a potter, I am far more impressed with the strength and vitality of the early works of the Geometric and Corinthian periods than I am by the later red-figured wares which are cold and hard in outline and have pictorial decorations that, although most skillfully executed, tend to float off the surface of the pieces.

The Greeks were originally a group of barbarian tribes from the north who gradually overran the peninsula from 1600 to 1100 B.C. and finally destroyed the Cretan kingdom. Thus, their early works reflect a Minoan and, to a lesser extent, an Egyptian influence. In periods like the Corinthian, a strong reflection of Mesopotamian design motifs is evident. Greek ceramists never used the flowering design, the colors, or the glazes so characteristic of the Minoans. The banded decoration of the early pieces with their delightfully stylized figures gradually gave way to one-panel designs fea-

Women Working Wool, Athenian lekythos of the black-figured style. Greece, ca. 560 B.C. Courtesy of The Metropolitan Museum of Art, Fletcher Fund, 1931.

A Victorious Charioteer and Nike, column krater in the red-figured style in which decoration becomes more detailed. Greece, ca. 460-450 B.C. Courtesy of The Metropolitan Museum of Art.

turing a single figure or a group of figures. The early Geometric ware (1100 to 700 B.C.) generally had a tan earthenware body and brown slip-like decoration. The Greeks never used a true glassy glaze. Their so-called "black-varnish" glaze was really a dark iron-bearing clay slip with added alkaline fluxes. As the Greeks were interested in rather detailed figure drawings, they did not use glazes which might run. This figure type of decoration was the natural outgrowth of the importance given athletic games in Greek culture. In fact, many vases served as prizes in these contests and were the forerunners of the trophies still being awarded today.

With pottery being such an accepted part of the culture, the various vase shapes became rather rigid types. The form of the vase became more mechanical. Since vases were used largely for decorative purposes, the Greeks added many nonfunctional features, such as flaring foot rims and sharp flat lips, which chipped and broke easily and are essentially more adapted to metal than clay. By 600 B.C. the prevailing style was the black-figured ware. This ware usually had a single banded panel with the figure in black against a red-clay background. The vase shown above (left) has a better feeling for form than the pieces made in the periods that followed and its decoration forms a pattern which stays on the pot. But the design of the foot displays a disregard for material which increased with time. Black-figured ware went out of style by about 520 B.C. when it was found that greater details could be achieved by using red figures against a black background (see above, right). The draftsmanship on many of these

Two views of a graceful and fragile red-figured kylix. Attica, Greece, ca. 490-480 B.C. Courtesy of The Metropolitan Museum of Art, Joseph Pulitzer Bequest, 1953.

pieces is excellent. The designs were not integrated with the curved surface of the vessel, however, and they are more appropriate for flat surfaces such as wall plaques. The kylix illustrated on this page is, none the less, an attractive piece, although it does not feel like a clay form to me. In fact, gold cups of a roughly similar design have been found.

The Greeks continued to develop pictorial designs on what was now a rather codified set of ceramic forms. A variation was the use of a white background with a rather lineal drawing. By the fourth century B.C. the "florid style," with its complex backgrounds, overcrowding of the panel, and use of colors, had evolved. The scenes depicted became sentimental or comic. After the arrival of the Romans, the decline continued, and Greek style achieved a vulgarity of ornateness unparalleled in ceramic history until the baroque and rococo period in Europe.

(Left) A Toltec pottery dog which serves as a bottle. Coloma, Mexico, ca. 800-1000. Courtesy of the Minneapolis Institute of Arts, Purchase, 1947: J. R. Van Derlip Fund. (Right) A freely modeled pre-Toltec figurine with an interesting bulbous quality. Tepic, Mexico, ninth to tenth centuries. Courtesy of the Chicago Natural History Museum.

Pre-Columbian Ceramics

When, as a pottery student, I first saw a large collection of pre-Columbian pottery, it was like the sound of strange music, so different was it from the ceramics of the Western world. Even the ceramics made by the Chinese, because of their intermittent trade for over a thousand years with the Middle East, are relatively familiar to us.

The pieces illustrated here date from roughly A.D. 1000. Two of the small sculptural pieces are from Mexico and the others are from Peru. Equally interesting pieces were made in other sections of North and South America. As a whole, the pre-Columbian pieces seem to be more plastic in feeling and have a more vital and vigorous quality than most Western or even Oriental ceramics. One reason for this difference may have been that the potter's wheel was unknown in the New World until the advent of the Spanish. All the pieces illustrated here were either built up entirely by hand or, more likely, pressed into a bisque mold by sections and later joined. These methods permit more varied approaches than are possible on the wheel.

The prevalence of the sculptural pot in the Mochica culture is perhaps a result of their physical environment. The Mochica tribes lived on the

(Right) Mochica stirrup pot, more of a sculptural achievement than pottery. Peru, ca. 1100. (Bottom, left) Chimu blackware stirrup pot in the shape of a puma. Peru, ca. 1000. (Bottom, right) Another Mochica stirrup pot, more potterylike in form, slip decoration. Peru, ca. 1100. All pieces on this page courtesy of The Art Institute of Chicago, Buckingham Fund.

Nazca earthenware bowl with a striking design derived from a row of trophy heads. Peru, ca. 1000. Courtesy of The Art Institute of Chicago, Buckingham Fund.

Feline goddess holding two trophy heads, Nazca stirrup pot with typical stylized design and highly burnished slip. Peru, 1000. Courtesy of The Art Institute of Chicago, Buckingham Fund.

Peruvian coastal plain which was largely desert. Streams cutting across the plains from the mountains made irrigation possible. With no source of plentiful wood or stone for sculpture they turned their efforts toward the ceramic medium. To look at many of the Mochica or Nazca pottery pieces with their variety of pastel hues, one would never believe that the New World Indians did not use a true silicious glaze. Their glazelike effects were achieved by the application of several coats of a finely ground slip which was later burnished when leather hard. The fine particle size, plus the forcing together of the clay mass, causes the clay molecules to fuse slightly in firing, thus producing a surface similar to a mat glaze. Of course, the ware was not waterproof. Like many pieces illustrated in this chapter, the Peruvian ceramics shown here were originally placed in burial chambers and had never been used.

Tzu-Chou pottery gallipot with brown decoration deftly applied over a cream glaze. China, Sung Dynasty, 960-1279. Courtesy of The Art Institute of Chicago, Gift of Russell Tyson.

Classic vase form with a sang-de-boeuf glaze so rich that it makes any decoration superfluous. China, Ch'ing Dynasty, 1662-1722. Courtesy of The Metropolitan Museum of Art.

Later Chinese Ceramics

The Chinese have the longest unbroken ceramic tradition in the world and one of unusually high quality. In the beginning of this chapter pieces were shown from several early periods. Despite a succession of wars and changes of dynasties the ceramic arts continued to develop and became one of the major art forms in China. Although always technically facile Chinese potters have seldom succumbed to the excesses so prevalent in European wares. They experimented with harder and higher-firing bodies and glazes. By approximately A.D. 250 they had learned to make an early type of porcelain, a feat not duplicated in Europe until nearly 1500 years later. Among their technical achievements are the copper-red and celadon glazes produced by a reduction firing of the kiln.

The Sung dynasty (960–1279) is regarded by many as the classic period of Chinese ceramics. Several pieces are illustrated here, all showing the strength and simplicity of form so characteristic of this age. The decoration relates beautifully to the shape of the pot and is executed with a sensitivity and vitality so seldom successfully combined. The other pieces shown were made during the reign of the first Ch'ing (Manchu) emperor, K'ang Hsi

White jar decorated with stylized flowers. China, Sung Dynasty, 960-1280. Courtesy of The Metropolitan Museum of Art.

Stoneware tea bowl with runny "Tenmoku" (hare's fur), felspathic glaze with a high iron content. China, Sung Dynasty, 960-1279. Courtesy of The Art Institute of Chicago, Buckingham Collection.

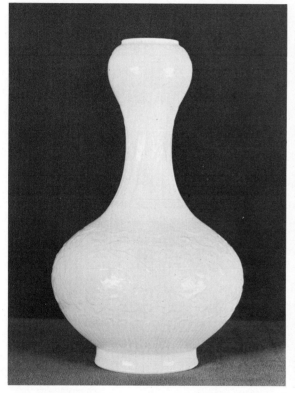

Gourd-shaped vase of thin porcelain with pressed design. The Ch'ing dynasty was a period of amazing technical competence guided by a still vital tradition. Emperor K'ang Hsi, 1662-1722. Courtesy of The Art Institute of Chicago, Buckingham Collection.

Porcelain Kwanyin figure with transparent greenish white glaze, 18½ inches high. China, Ch'ing Dynasty, Emperor K'ang Hsi, 1662-1722. Courtesy of The Art Institute of Chicago, Buckingham Collection.

(1662–1722), following the famous Ming period. The sang-de-boeuf vase (see p. 164), with its rubylike glaze, reflects the monumental quality of earlier ages and is a most handsome piece. The porcelain pieces have an elegance not previously achieved, yet they are not weak in form.

Panel of enameled brick from the famous Lion Wall built by King Nebuchadnezzar II (605-562 B.C.) in Babylon. Courtesy of The Metropolitan Museum of Art.

Persian Ceramics

While we mentioned them briefly in connection with Crete, we have, for lack of space, neglected the considerable ceramic arts developed in Mesopotamia. A portion of a glazed brick wall lining a processional street in Babylon, shown on this page, is indicative of the work produced in an early period. The pottery illustrated dates from the eighth to the seventeenth centuries.

Chinese ceramics, particularly the porcelains, were imported into the Middle East as early as the T'ang dynasty (618–906). Porcelain was highly prized and Middle Eastern potters searched for its secret. Although they never discovered the secret, they came up with a half-way solution: A lead-tin glaze was developed which gave a white color to earthenware.

As a result of a religious edict which forbade human representation and their training in calligraphy, Islamic potters developed amazing skill in curvilinear decoration. In spite of the intricacy of their designs, the over-all effect is seldom crowded or disorderly. The highest development of lusterware is an achievement of Islamic potters, although luster glazes were also used at an early period in Egypt. The metallic sheens of gold, silver, and purple fitted perfectly into the elaborately decorative nature of their work. The widespread use of glazed tiles in mosques, gardens, and private homes was another unique feature of Persian ceramics.

Kashan lusterware wall tile of the type used in both religious and private buildings. Persia, eighth century. Courtesy of The Metropolitan Museum of Art.

Pottery plate with stylized floral designs. Turkey, early seventeenth century. Courtesy of The Metropolitan Museum of Art, Rogers Fund, 1928.

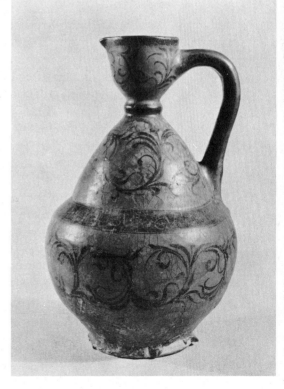

(Left) Rhages bowl decorated with golden luster. Persia, twelfth century. Courtesy of The Metropolitan Museum of Art, Rogers Fund, 1920. (Right) Sultanabad ewer, buff earthenware with a transparent turquoise glaze. Persia, thirteenth to fourteenth centuries. Courtesy of The Art Institute of Chicago, Mr. and Mrs. Martin A. Ryerson Collection.

Hispano-Moresque lusterware plate. Valencia, Spain, sixteenth century. Courtesy of The Metropolitan Museum of Art, Bequest of Mrs. H. O. Havemeyer, 1929. H. O. Havemeyer Collection.

Majolica armory plate, low fired body with lead-tin glaze. Florence, Italy, ca. 1480. Courtesy of The Metropolitan Museun of Art.

Spain and Renaissance Italy

During the Middle Ages even the decadent pottery skills of the Romans were lost to Italy. The revival of pottery making in Europe came from an entirely unexpected source. With the Moslem conquest of North Africa and much of Spain came the considerable skills of the Islamic potter. During the early Renaissance the prospering commercial centers of Italy imported pottery from Spain. This pottery, generally but not always lusterware, is properly called Hispano-Moresque ware, but because the trading vessels from Spain generally stopped en route at Majorca, all tin-enameled wares came to be called "majolica."

The revival of Italian ceramics was rather short lived. With the success of the Renaissance painter the potter also turned to painting, at first clumsily, as seen in the quaint Jonah and whale on this page. The realistic sketch on the albarello on page 169 was only the beginning. Soon large plates were entirely covered with religious and mythological scenes. Their foot rims were fitted with holes for hanging. Like Picasso's plates they were made to serve as pictures, not as pottery.

One interesting development in this period was the work of the della Robbia family. Ceramic sculpture had been made for some time in Italy. Most of it was gilded and polychromed after firing. Although not the first to glaze such sculpture, Lucca della Robbia (1400?–1482) was perhaps

Majolica albarello, decorated in more forceful manner than usual for the period. Faenza, Italy, ca. 1475. Courtesy of The Metropolitan Museum of Art.

Madonna and Child with Scroll, terra cotta with lead-tin glaze. Lucca della Robbia. Italy, fifteenth century. Courtesy of The Metropolitan Museum of Art.

the first to do it successfully. The lead-tin glaze he used gave the impression of white marble although this may not have been his intention. Lucca founded a family business which continued for several generations, but unfortunately none of his successors had his ability as a sculptor. Not only were these later figures poorly modeled but gaudy glazes were used which greatly distracted from the sculptural form. Lucca's work was not inferior to sculptors of his period who were working in other mediums.

Early English Pottery

Little pottery of the eighteenth and nineteenth centuries in Europe has much esthetic merit, but before the period of the mass-production factory many interesting things were made. Of particular interest is the English pottery of the twelfth to fourteenth centuries, particularly the simple pots made for daily use and glazed only on the inside. Perhaps the most handsome pieces are the tall cylindrical jugs with their bulbous forms and strong pulled handles.

Patio lamp, off-white glaze with unglazed earthenware bands. Carl Paak.

CHAPTER 12

STUDIO EQUIPMENT*

Ceramic Kilns

The essential item and the most expensive piece of ceramic equipment is the
kiln. It is possible to make a variety of pottery and sculptural ceramic
forms without using any of the equipment listed here except a kiln. Since
the kiln is the most important and costly purchase, it is advisable to select
the type and size which will fit both present and future needs.

SIZE and USE. Since we are not concerned with commercial mass-
production methods, our choices of kilns are limited to the small or
moderate-sized intermittent types. Economy of operation is a factor if the
kiln is used in a private studio which is supported by the sale of the items
produced. On the other hand, in a school, ease of loading and freedom
from maintenance are factors of equal importance. In any case, the small
hobby-type kilns so often found in public schools and colleges are too small
to take care of the output of the class or studio. The few small items which
can be fired in such kilns are not worth the time it takes to tend them.
These kilns are often advertized as test kilns, but they are not good for
testing purposes. *The heat rise in a test kiln must be as slow and as uniform as
that of a large kiln if the samples are to have the same maturing temperature and
surface qualities.* Unless especially constructed, the average small kiln heats
up and cools off too rapidly to test glazes which will normally be fired in a
larger kiln.

The Harrop electric kiln illustrated on page 172 has a firing chamber
18 x 18 x 15 inches, the minimum size that I would recommend for the

* The manufacturers of all equipment illustrated in this chapter plus many other firms will be
found listed in the Appendix. The prices listed are those in effect on the date of publication.
Schools may usually obtain an educational discount.

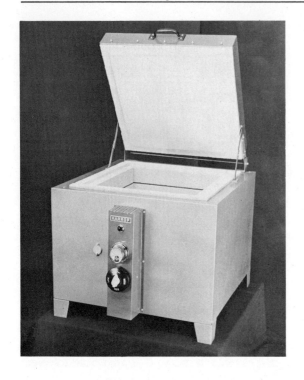

Harrop top-loading electric kiln for temperatures to 2000°F; 18 x 18 x 15″ kiln chamber. Price FOB Columbus, Ohio, $153.00, without pyrometer. (Measurements given indicate height, width, and depth.)

average school studio. It is suitable for cone-04 glazes and bodies which are satisfactory for public school and beginning college classes. For the college program it is desirable to have in addition at least one gas kiln which will fire to cones 8 to 12, not only for the higher temperatures that can be achieved but also for the reduction effects permitted.

There is a greater economy of operation if the gas kiln is not too small. A 3-cubic-foot kiln, depending upon comparative fuel costs, might be cheaper to fire by electricity. But as the size increases, the cost per cubic foot drops. The relationship between the bulk of the fire brick to be heated and the volume of the chamber makes larger kilns more economical to operate. Even though a kiln which will take most of a semester's work in one firing may be economical, it is not the most educational. Frequent firings help the student to experiment and profit by his errors. The loading and firing procedures are a part of pottery making in which the beginner needs training.

A kiln with a firing chamber 18 x 18 x 15 inches is large enough for the average college class (15) of beginning students. Using this rather small kiln will necessitate frequent firings—about two per week and more toward the end of the semester. For a class of advanced students, a kiln this size is inadequate. For the sake of flexibility, perhaps two kilns of this size would be preferable to a larger one. Since ceramics is usually one of the

Harrop front-loading floor kiln for temperatures to 2000°F; kiln chamber, 18 x 18 x 19″. Price, FOB Columbus, Ohio, $607.73; with automatic controls, $857.00. Other models for temperatures to 2300°F available.

more popular courses, appealing to general college as well as art students, it is best not to limit the kiln size too closely but to allow for a certain amount of flexibility in load size.

Classes of 30 to 45 beginning and advanced students can be accomodated with two 3-cubic-foot cone-8 electric kilns and a 12-foot cone-12 gas kiln. Firings, of course, must be frequent. A workshop system can be established. An assistant to the instructor can take charge of loading and firing the kiln so that a continuous flow of ware can go through the kiln room. These suggestions assume that the class is producing quality ware and spending a certain amount of time on experimental pieces. If the class were merely slip casting simple ash trays, three times the above kiln capacity would be necessary.

Top versus Front Loaders

The question of which type of kiln to purchase bothers most prospective kiln owners. There are definite advantages to each one. These are not constant values, however; they depend largely upon the size of the kiln desired. Price, too, is a factor. A top loader, for example, is less costly to construct. No heavy framework or hinge to support a heavy swinging door is necessary. If the heat is to be uniform in an electric kiln, elements will have to be installed in the door. The extra connections involved make this more expensive. The permanent roof of the kiln chamber is more trouble-some to construct than the flat cover of a top loader which can be cheaply replaced. On the other hand, unless the cover of the top loader is well constructed and fitted, there will be greater heat loss through the top than through the door of a front loader. Since heat tends to rise, the kiln should have separate controls for the top and bottom series of elements. When the top cone melts, the top elements may be turned to medium until the bottom temperature equalizes. Shelves should not be placed extremely low or just under the cover in an electric kiln. Unless there are elements in the floor or the cover, the center of these areas generally has a cool spot. A wider spacing of the shelves will allow better heat circulation.

In the smaller size, the top loader is definitely easier to load and more economical. The potter can use both hands to position the ware and can accurately judge the clearance between the pieces. The shelves are easy to place. Top-loading gas kilns are also made, although they are not as common as the electric models. Since the hot gases in these models pass around all sides of the kiln chamber, the heat is more uniform than in the usual kiln which has a muffle on each side.

The point at which depth becomes a problem will depend upon the individual potter. I prefer a top loader up to a depth of 20 inches. After that, I find that the convenience of the front loader is worth the extra price. Very few top loaders, however, are made deeper than 24 inches. Their average depth is from 15 to 18 inches.

There are occasions when the depth (15 to 18 inches) of the top loader is an inconvenience. Quite frequently a tall bottle or a piece of sculpture cannot be fired. To handle this situation, I have built two sections to add on to the kiln which give it an additional 15 inches in depth. These are, in effect, kilns without tops or bottoms. They are placed upon the kiln and the regular kiln cover is used on top. By means of metal pins and angle-iron frames with take-up bolts, the insulating bricks are held firm enough to be lifted off and on when necessary. A heating element is placed in each section and plugged in like a hot plate.

THE ELECTRIC KILN has many advantages. Gas lines are not always available and the chimneys are seldom adequate to carry off the extremely hot exhaust gases. There is, in addition, the danger of explosion if care is not taken during the initial lighting and firing of a gas kiln. If anything goes wrong during the firing of an electric kiln, however, it merely blows a fuse. Smaller-sized electric kilns can run on 110 volts, but those large enough to be practical need 220 volts with an installation similar to that of an electric stove. There are three basic types of elements available for electric kilns. The most common is the nickel-nichrome coiled wire which is used in most kilns firing up to 2000°F. Kanthal elements are available in strip or wire for temperatures to 2300°F (cone 8). An even higher-firing electric kiln, with the trade name of Globar, uses elements which are in a square or round rod form composed of a carborundum material. Extremely high temperatures are possible with this type of kiln (up to 2700°F). Needless to say, it is much too expensive for the average school or studio. Its chief uses are for experimental work in metal alloys, in metal heat treatments, and in the production of a variety of high-fired porcelain products which are primarily used as electrical insulators. The Globar kiln also needs a special transformer which further prohibits its use in the public school or typical studio.

If not overfired these various types of electrical elements will give very good service before replacement is necessary. I have frequently used elements for more than a year which had been fired an average of three times per week. Normally, the cost of completely replacing elements for low-fire kilns is slightly less than 10 percent of the original kiln cost. For high-fire models, the replacement cost is greater and may be from 15 percent to nearly 25 percent of the kiln cost. These come, however, in units of from 3 to 10 per kiln. Under normal circumstances, the elements will never all burn out together.

A comparison of the electric models of various manufacturers reveals a considerable price difference between models firing at low temperatures of 2000°F and those intended for operation at between 2300° and 2400°F. As noted above there is a large price differential in the cost of the elements. Most of the added cost, however, is due to the greater thickness, the better quality of the insulating material, and the heavier electrical system and steel framework required. For the hobbyist who only fires a couple times a month the low-firing kiln may be satisfactory. However, even though the final firing temperature may never go above 1950°F (cone 04), the higher-firing kiln (2300°F) is preferable for a school where frequent firings are necessary. Two years of steady firing such as encountered in a college class, will just about burn out an inexpensive low-fire kiln even though it is never overfired. On the other hand, the Kanthal-wired kiln, because of its better construction, will still be in good condition.

Nickel-nichrome elements have a tendency to contract after repeated firings and may pull out of the recesses in the kiln wall. Unless the wire has become brittle from overfiring, it can be stretched out and put back in

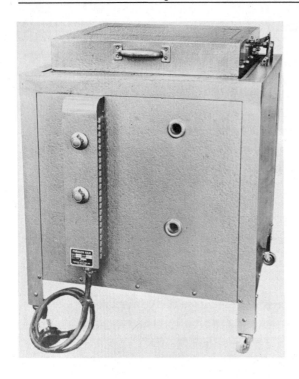

Paragon top-loading electric kiln for temperatures to 2300°F (cone 8); kiln chamber, 17 x 17 x 18″.   Price FOB Dallas, Tex., $287.50.

place. On the other hand, Kanthal-type elements become very brittle after firing and should not be touched in any way. If they are not fired above cone 04, however, a contraction similar to that of nickel-nichrome elements will take place. Firing Kanthal wire to cone 8 will serve to set and keep it in place; after such a firing lower firings will not affect the wire. Next to overfiring the greatest source of element damage results from the rapid heating and explosion of a glazed piece or the careless chipping and cleaning of glaze drippings from the kiln floor. If particles of glaze touch the elements, they will burn out after a few firings.

Such an accident occurred to me several years ago. I had constructed an electric kiln using 2600°F bricks and Kanthal elements which were recessed into grooves in the bricks. The elements burned out. I thought that the wiring hookup was faulty until I discovered that iron impurities melted out of the bricks and caused the Kanthal wire to burn out. This never happened to me with the nickel-nichrome elements, doubtless because the iron impurities did not melt until 2200°F.

Care should be exercised in choosing materials when the potter wants to build his own kiln. Depending upon the type of kiln and the ability of the builder, a comparable kiln can be built at about one-half of the retail price. It is advisable to try to more or less duplicate a successful kiln on the market. The proportions between chamber area and element size are critical. Most of the homemade kilns which I have seen perform inadequately for this reason. After designing the kiln, the major steps are getting a steel frame welded and procuring proper electrical switches. Wiring may require the advice of an electrician. For a low-fire kiln, 2300°F insulating bricks are satisfactory and they are available from most building-supply houses. They can be cut easily with a hack-saw blade.

Replacement elements come coiled up like screen-door springs and must be stretched out to fit the length of the recess. Drive four nails into a plywood panel at distances similar to the channel recess. Then stretch out the element wire until it will make the correct number of turns around the nails. Bend the wire sharply at the corners but do not allow the spirals to touch at any place. Then take out the nails and transfer the square-shaped elements to the recesses in the kiln. On rare occasions when an element breaks near a terminal connection, it may be stretched out and made to work a while longer. If the break is near the middle, however, the element will heat up too much to last long.

Mention has been made of reduction firings in gas kilns. Pine splinters or moth balls should not be inserted in electric kilns to reduce glaze coloring oxides or the body. The Kanthal manufacturers advise against firing in a reduction atmosphere. However, a potter of my acquaintance has for many years finished off his firing with a reduction by allowing fuel oil to drip into the kiln chamber after the cone was down and the current turned off. This is not the best time to reduce. Normally reduction should start at the point when the first glaze ingredients start to react, about cone 016, depending in part upon the type of glaze used. In the case just mentioned, however, the final reduction does have some effect on body and glaze color, but not in the manner of a standard reduction. Since the current is turned off before reduction, the chemical reaction, if any, is not as pronounced. Apparently no harm has been done to the elements.

GAS KILNS, because of the greater care necessary in the firing procedure, are not recommended for public-school use. For a college program, however, a gas kiln is essential not only to take care of the larger production but to allow for higher temperatures and reduction methods.

The kiln should not be so large as to handicap experimentation nor should it be so small as to hamper production or limit expansion of the program. As in the case of the electric kiln, the top loader is a more economical model to purchase. In the smaller sizes it is easier to load and generally produces a more uniform distribution of heat. In the front-loading models particular attention should be paid to door size and to kiln depth versus kiln width. The newer kiln models have doors which open to the full width of the chamber. In some cases the depth of the kiln is less than the door size, the reverse of many older models; this greatly facilitates kiln loading.

The gas coming into the building must come through adequately sized pipes and have sufficient pressure. The bare minimum requirements may prove to be insufficient during peak heating periods and the final cones may never go over. The other requirement for a gas installation is a sound chimney. The exhaust gases from a kiln are considerably hotter than from a heating furnace. The pipe connection between the kiln and chimney must have a standard fire-clay inner lining. Some kilns do not have a direct pipe connection but have instead a hood over the kiln. In this case, the exhaust gases are not quite so hot since a good deal of the cooler air from the room is pulled into the hood from the draft of the stack. If the kiln is installed in a shed or on an upper floor of a building, it is possible to use transite (a pressed cement-asbestos pipe) for a chimney provided there is air space around it.

Most gas kilns used today are muffle kilns, which means that the ware is placed in a separate chamber. The flame and hot gases of the combustion pass below, above, and on two or four sides of the chamber. To have a reduction fire in this case it is necessary to take off the top muffle panel as well as part of the side panels. If the kiln is well designed, it should be possible to vary the fire from oxidizing to reducing by adjusting the air and gas. Usually a slight reduction will not harm glazes. If a manufactured gas is used, however, its sulphur by-product will affect some lead glazes.

It is most beneficial for the life of a kiln to heat it up slowly. This is more important for gas kilns than for electric models. The kiln floor and supports of gas kilns must necessarily be made of heavy refractory materials which are affected more by heat expansion than the more porous outer shell of the insulating brick in electric kilns. It is equally advisable to close the draft or chimney vents as soon as the gas is turned off in order to prevent a cold draft of air from being sucked into the hot combustion chamber. This is the weak spot in any fuel-burning kiln. Eventually floor sections and supports will have to be replaced. This is not too difficult a job. Much depends upon the type and condition of the kiln. Cracks, of course, will have to be repaired from time to time with a refractory kiln cement. Major repairs can be largely avoided if reasonable care is exercised in operating the kiln.

OTHER TYPES OF KILNS are made to suit a variety of fuel or firing

Dickinson front-loading natural-draft gas kiln for temperatures to cone 6; 12-cubic-foot kiln chamber, 29 x 24 x 30". Price FOB Los Angeles, Calif., $1550.00; crating $30.00. Other models to cone 12.

Apine forced-draft front-loading gas kiln for temperatures to 2500°F with automatic cut-off controls; 20-cubic-foot kiln chamber, measures 32 x 24 x 46". Price FOB Culver City, Calif., $1832.00.

conditions. In most areas bottled gas is competitive in price with other fuels which can be substituted for natural gas. Its greater convenience is an advantage unless the price is prohibitive. A kiln similar to the gas kiln can be fired with fuel oil. As in the case of the gas kiln, the fuel oil can be used with either a natural- or a forced-draft burner. Except for its greater cleanliness, gas is not very different from other fuels.

In past years, coal- and wood-burning kilns were commonly used. They must be moderately large for school purposes (over 30 cubic feet) to be efficient. The firing time is much longer and requires experienced handling. Many people find it difficult to start a fire in a fireplace, let alone a kiln fire. A small pottery outside of Copenhagen, Saxbo Stoneware, still uses a large coal kiln, and it is not an old kiln. It takes about three days to fire, and it produces the finest porcelain and stoneware. The Ateneum (art academy) of Helsinki has a large wood kiln. It, too, takes a while to fire, but it produced fine ware. Perhaps in America we are too concerned with convenience.

Salt kilns are about as rare as wood-burning kilns. In fact a salt kiln may be wood-fired. The salt glaze is produced by throwing common table

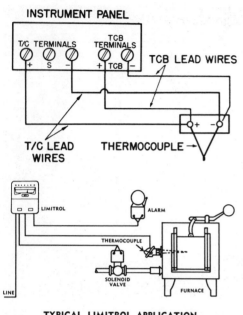

TYPICAL LIMITROL APPLICATION

Diagram of Wheelco Limitrol heat-control instruments suitable for larger kiln installations.

Barber-Colman automatic shut-off for both gas and electric kilns, for temperatures to 2500°F. Prices from $185.00.

salt (sodium chloride) into the firebox or special ports in the kiln when the body is mature. The salt combines with the silica of the body, generally a stoneware body, to form a durable glaze. The salt glaze was more common during the eighteenth and nineteenth centuries than it is at present. The single firing is an advantage, and colored slips and body stains can be used under the glaze. The disadvantage of the salt kiln is that nothing else can be fired in it with certainty, since the entire kiln interior tends to be coated with the rather volatile glaze.

When a kiln is purchased, it generally comes supplied with very minimal kiln furniture. The term *kiln furniture* refers to the shelves and the shelf supports and the various types of supports for glazed ware. It will be necessary to purchase additional shelves. When purchasing a small quantity, it is more convenient to buy from the kiln manufacturer than from a manufacturer of refractories. Fire-clay shelves for kilns up to 2000°F are quite satisfactory and more economical than silicon-carbide shelves, which should be used for temperatures above 2200°F. It is possible to use fire-clay shelves at these higher temperatures but they must have greater thickness to avoid warping. Fluted supports with hollow cores are very satisfactory. In time the edges will get chipped, causing them to rock. When they do, fluted supports should be ground down on an emery wheel in sets of four. Insulating bricks may also be cut down to serve as supports

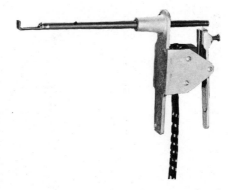

Kiln Joy automatic cut-off for electric cones, using pyrometric cones to trigger switch action. Mason Instrument Co. Price: 110 volts, $17.95; 220 volts, $26.90.

where the kiln load tends to be rather light, as it generally is in a school situation.

HEAT-CONTROL DEVICES are a great help in a school situation where there are many distractions and perhaps more than one person tending the kiln. The usual type of heat control consists of a very accurate pyrometer with an adjustable pointer which permits the kiln to be turned off at a set temperature. The control problem is less complicated in an electric kiln since it only requires the interruption of the current. A gas kiln requires the installation of a solenoid valve in the gas line; the valve is electrically activated and turns off the gas flow as easily as the electric current. Gas kilns should also be supplied with a warning bell which will sound off to warn the potter to close the chimney flues, thus preventing the kiln from cooling off too rapidly.

All gas kilns should be installed with safety valves which will automatically turn off the gas supply if the burner flame goes out. With proper installation and reasonable care, the gas kiln is perfectly safe to operate. If the school program allows for a 8- to 16-cubic-foot kiln, it should be purchased. The expense of most automatic control equipment ($150 to $200 and up plus installation) has largely limited their use to the larger kilns which, because of the initial investment and the capacity involved, justify the extra cost. In the past few years, several inexpensive shut-off devices, priced from about $18 to $35 (see figure above), have appeared on the market for smaller-sized electric kilns. Two particular brands, Kiln Joy and Kiln Gard, are operated by the bending of a pyrometric cone which releases a spring electrical contact, thereby interrupting the current. Since these devices use small cones, the difference in maturing temperatures between these and the larger size must be noted (see Appendix). Care must be taken to keep the movable metal parts free from corrosion as a little fouling will interfere with accurate operation. These devices are best used with regular cones as safety features rather than alone as the sole control elements.

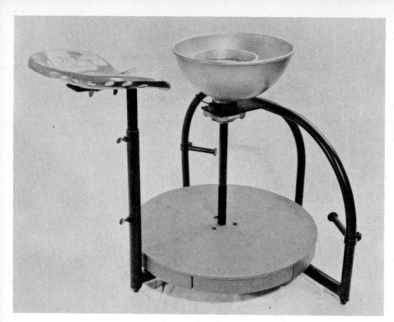

(Left) Randall kick wheel, welded construction, adjustable seat, and long-running 115-lb wheel plate. (Right) Power attachment for Randall wheel, $\frac{1}{3}$-hp motor. Prices FOB Alfred, N.Y.: wheel, $225.00; attachment, $98.00.

Potter's Wheels

Almost as indispensable as the kiln is the potter's wheel. While it is true that many fine and unusual pieces can be made by hand, wheel pieces will always constitute the major production. There are many types of potter's wheels, probably none of which are much different from the first one made about 6000 years ago. Eastern and Mideastern models are sunk into the ground and the potter squats over them when he throws. All Western types are made for throwing while the potter is standing or sitting.

Concerning the best type of wheel, there are almost as many ideas as there are potters. I have come to believe that choice is largely the result of a potter's accidental contact with a particular model. For the convenience of the reader several different types of wheels made in various sections of the country are illustrated. While each potter will develop his own preference, it is desirable to expose a student to various models so that he may become proficient upon them all.

THE SIMPLE KICK WHEEL is a direct descendant of primitive man's original model. The wheel illustrated on this page, with its welded-pipe frame and spun-alumilite drip pan, is a very modern offspring. Despite its rather unusual appearance, it is a very efficient and practical wheel, and most comfortable to use, particularly if the potter is throwing for a number of hours. The wheel is heavy enough to run without being constantly kicked. Control over speed is easily maintained by the foot while the hands are kept on the work. Tall pieces can be easily thrown—because the throwing head is low—between one's knees in fact.

Abernathy kick wheel, welded construction, 75-lb flywheel (pan removed). Price FOB Ann Arbor, Mich., $185.00.

Soldner kick wheel, welded "X" frame, adjustable seat, reinforced-concrete, 55-lb flywheel (heavier wheel available). Price FOB Claremont, Calif., $175.00; six or more $150.00.

Littleton side-kick wheel, welded construction; 14″ aluminum wheel head removable for easy cleaning of fiberglass pan; 75-lb flywheel. Price FOB Verona, Wis., $175.00.

Abernathy side-kick wheel, welded steel construction with large work pan. Price FOB Ann Arbor, Mich., $185.00.

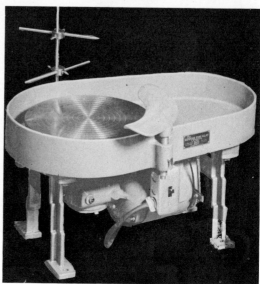

Crossley variable-speed wheel and jigger, an industrial model with ¾-hp electric motor and speeds from 0 to 525 rpm; weight, 475 lb. Price FOB Trenton, N.J., $855.65.

D.F.C. electric wheel, with ¼-hp 110-volt (AC) motor, variable speeds for 80 to 200 rpm, and 12″ wheel head. Price FOB Denver, Colo., $317.80.

THE SIDE-KICK WHEEL is a development or rather a modification of the standard simple wheel. The use of an off-center pin and a push bar, eliminates the need for a heavy flywheel. However, the weight (75 lb) of the Littleton flywheel (see p. 183) makes it heavy enough to run for a while and allows the body to remain rigid during the more critical part of throwing. The large work pan is conveniently removable for cleaning. The wheel may be operated from a standing position or while the potter is seated on a tall stool.

All of the kick wheels illustrated were designed by potters for use in their own studios or classrooms and are made to order by local machine shops. Their sturdy welded construction is a pleasant change from the flimsy items which have generally been manufactured.

ELECTRIC WHEELS have advantages under certain circumstances. I believe that the student should learn to throw upon the kick wheel where quick changes in speed are not possible. For the skilled potter doing production throwing the use of an electric wheel is practically a necessity to avoid excessive fatigue. An electric wheel, to be of any value, must be capable of truly variable speed adjustments. Furthermore, it must be able to furnish adequate power at low speeds. The wheels illustrated are not inexpensive. The Crossley model is intended as a factory-production jigger as well as a throwing model. Before buying a wheel the potter is advised to try it himself and not depend upon advertizing claims. Care-

Advanced electric wheel with $\frac{1}{2}$-hp 110/220-volt (AC–DC) motor, variable speeds from 0 to 120 rpm, forward or reverse. Price FOB Los Angeles, Calif., for motor unit with 14″ cast-aluminum-alloy throwing head, $295.00; with 24 x 30″ table, welded frame, $325.00.

fully compare motors and reduction gear types. Some gear arrangements give much more power at lower speeds with less wear. In my experience wheels using rubber pulleys for speed adjustments are not satisfactory.

Glaze-room Equipment

Glaze-room equipment includes spray machines and booths, mortars, sieves, and ball mills. The amount and type of equipment will vary greatly according to the potting situation.

SCHOOL EQUIPMENT in the lower grades or at the junior-high-school level may be extremely simple. Glazing at this level usually consists of brushing or pouring which eliminates the need for spray gun and booth. On occasions a mortar, a pestle, and a 45- or 60-mesh sieve may prove helpful in reclaiming a jar with a dry or lumpy glaze.

SPRAY EQUIPMENT in the high school or college must include a spray booth if glaze spraying is contemplated since lead glazes are extremely toxic. Illustrated is a small spray booth with an exhaust fan and glass wool fitters (on p. 186). By soaking in warm water the trapped glaze may be reclaimed for use again. An inexpensive galvanized booth can be constructed in the school shop. If a proper direct exhaust is available, filters

(Left) Craftool ceramic spray booth, 24 x 24 x 28″, complete with 10″ electric exhaust fan and glass wool filters. Price FOB New York, N.Y., $125.00; without stand, $115.00; air filter and regulator, $18.95. (Top, right) Lightweight spray outfit with compressor, $\frac{1}{4}$-hp motor, gun, and jar. American Art Clay Co. Price $67.50. (Bottom, right) Brass hand sprayer for small pieces. American Art Clay Co. Price $5.75.

are unnecessary. While spraying uses more glaze, much of the excess can be reclaimed from the booth walls. The brass hand sprayer illustrated on this page should not be confused with the ordinary dime-store fly sprayer. This model develops a continuous pressure and is satisfactory for small amounts of work in a home studio.

There are a number of inexpensive spray machines made for paint and various utility purposes which will work adequately in the high school or college spray room. Many schools with shops have compressed air available which would eliminate the need for a compressor. Compressors are noisy and if they are used, the motor should be sound proofed. An inexpensive sprayer may be improvised with an ordinary fixative sprayer attached to the air line.

(Left) Standard equipment for every studio. American Art Clay Co. Prices: sieves, $5.50 to $7.25; mortar and pestles, $3.95 to $7.90; decoration wheels, $5.75 to $15.00.

(Right) Craftool porcelain ball-mill jars. Prices FOB New York, N.Y.: gallon jar, $32.00; half-gallon jar, $19.50; quart jar, $16.50; pebbles extra.

GLAZE-MIXING EQUIPMENT need not be very complicated in the average high school or college situation. Most glaze materials in common use today are so finely ground that actual grinding is unnecessary. A small amount of glaze (for example a quart) may be mixed with water in a jar with an ordinary wooden dowel. Larger amounts up to a gallon or two may be easily mixed or stirred up after they have settled in a minute or two with a portable electric kitchen mixer.

Occasionally glazes, particularly raw borax glazes, become hard or lumpy in a jar and may need to be ground with a *mortar* and *pestle*. In fact, such glazes usually must be ground originally in the mortar and pestle and even then they are too coarse to spray easily. In our studio we reclaim all the glaze deposited on the spray booths plus the odds and ends left in the glaze storage jars. Since this is often quite a mixture of lumpy particles, we usually put it all into a *ball-mill* jar and grind it for a couple of hours in order to get a sample to fire. The gallon size is the most useful jar to have although on occasion smaller ones are handy. Mill jars are fairly standard. Many manufacturers make them and the only difference seems to be in the clamp arrangement which holds the cover on. A new type which has a plastic screw on its cover is much cheaper than the others.

Craftool roller-type ball mill, two-gallon size. Price FOB New York, N.Y., $44.50; motor extra.

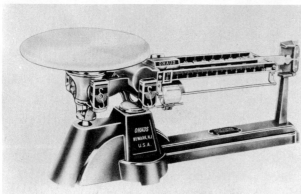

Ohaus triple-beam gram scale; several models available from local dealers. Price for model illustrated, $19.50.

There are several methods used to rotate the jars. Some clamp in a frame which spins. The most common rotator is the roller type illustrated on this page. This model is shown without the motor which turns the rollers and thus the mill. When ordering them, make certain that the rollers are long enough to take two one-gallon jars. Many larger mills having several banks of rollers are on the market for use in experimental laboratories. For most school studios, however, a double-gallon mill is sufficient. The charge of grinding balls may be either porcelain or flint pebbles. A variation in size is preferable in order to secure better grinding action. Sufficiently accurate *gram scales* can be purchased at every ceramic supply house for about $20. It is advisable to have at least two scales in the studio and extra 500 gram weights are useful. For compounding clay bodies a balance scale which will handle up to 100 pounds is most helpful.

Brass-bound sieves with bronze wire should be included in the studio equipment for sieving clay and glazes. They are numbered according to the number of openings per lineal inch. Recommended sizes would be a #15 for sieving clay and grog and a #45, #60, and #80 for glazes.

Dickinson shuttle kiln, 50-cubic-foot chamber; over-all length, 20′. Smaller 16′ studio model has a chamber 24 x 45 x 25″; crated weight, 6000 lb. Price FOB Los Angeles, Calif., for 16′ model: for cone 04, $2200.00; for cone 6, $2300.00; for cone 12, $2600.00.

Special Equipment

Most of the items described here are not found in the typical college ceramic studio, but with the increasing interest in ceramics some of these so-called special items may soon become as important as the wheel or the kiln. The first item which I would like to discuss is a special kiln.

SHUTTLE KILNS are widely used commercially in small- to medium-sized potteries. As can be seen in the figure above, a shuttle kiln is essentially a kiln with a door on each end. There are two floors which roll in and out of the kiln on a track. It is more convenient and faster to load than the conventional kiln. Furthermore there is a saving of fuel since one load can be pulled out and a new load pushed into the still-quite-warm kiln. Its widespread commercial use would indicate its practicality. Models are available as small as 16 cubic feet. The kiln illustrated has a capacity of 50 cubic feet. Because of its open-fire type of construction its cost is not as high as might be expected. Any studio or department normally firing about three times per week may find the shuttle kiln worthwhile considering.

International Clay Machinery Co. laboratory pug mill, with tub 9" x 4'; capacity, 1500-2000 lbs in 8 hours; weight, 300 lb. Price FOB Dayton, Ohio, $995.00.

St. Paul Studio pug mill, 58" x 30" x 21"; capacity, 200-300 lbs per hour. Price FOB St. Paul, Minn., for mill with $1\frac{1}{2}$-hp single-phase motor, $634.79, shipping weight, 375 lb; without motor, $267.93, shipping weight, 220 lb.

THE PUG MILL is another item seldom found in the ceramic studio. In any fair-sized department it is a most welcome equipment addition. Several models are illustrated here. The pug mill is a troughlike hopper into which either water and dry clay or moist clay scraps are placed. Knifelike blades on a revolving shaft cut and compress the clay until it is a homogeneous mass. Then a screwlike attachment on one end discharges the clay in a round or oval form, much as one would squeeze a tube of toothpaste. Studio-sized pug mills will generally mix from 200 to 300 pounds of plastic clay an hour in a section 2 to 3 inches in diameter. This clay is normally just a trifle moist to throw but it can be aged for a couple weeks and wedged. The pug mill saves the labor and time involved in pounding up old dry lumps, soaking up scraps, and batting up soupy clay slips.

A BLUNGER is essentially a king-sized mixmaster which is used commercially to mix large quantities of glaze or casting slips. It is equipped with a clamp which can be fastened to a large galvanized can or a wooden barrel. In the studio without a pug mill, the blunger may be used to blend water with dry clays or soft small clay scraps. Clay prepared in this way must, of course, be placed in bats. It is convenient to store the clay in

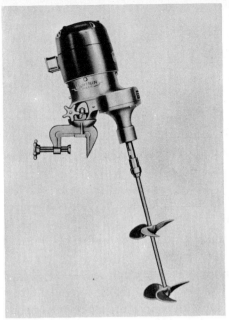

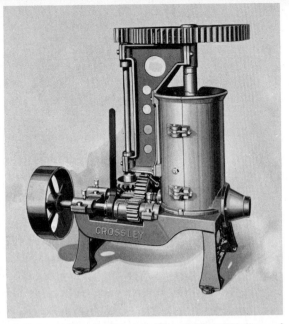

Mixing Equipment Co. "Lightnin" blunger; models from $\frac{1}{8}$ to 3 hp. The smaller sizes are adequate for the studio. Prices FOB Rochester, N.Y., from $150.00 to $600.00.

Crossley 12″ vertical pug mill, weighing 780 lbs and requiring 3-hp motor; can deliver a pugged clay section 3″ in diameter at a rate of 18″ per minute. Price FOB Trenton, N.J., $1600.00; motor extra.

several large cans to allow it to settle; then the excess water can be siphoned off before batting.

A FILTER PRESS is an accordionlike machine made of metal and canvas. It is filled with clay slip under pressure and compressed. The water seeps out through the canvas. When the clay has reached the desired moisture content, the sections are uncoupled and the clay removed in flat slabs. In addition to the press, a blunger, a screen, and a clay pressure pump are necessary to complete the installation. Its expense is justified only when perfectly pure and homogeneous bodies are needed for experimental purposes in such fields as electronics. The pug mill fulfills the studio potter's need more efficiently and less expensively.

MILL GRINDERS and POT FURNACES are valuable only for experimental work in frits and color stains. Frits and stains may be made on a small scale in a crucible placed in a regular kiln and later broken up with a mortar and pestle and then ball milled. Normally, mill grinders and frit furnaces are available only in ceramic engineering departments which do considerable work in frits, stains, and special glazes. In this case a mill which will grind to a fine particle size is not a convenience but a necessity. Some frits are easily broken up after being calcined. Others cool into a solid crystalline mass which can only be released by breaking the crucible. Needless to say, this makes the grinding process much more difficult. A frit pot furnace will allow the frits to be poured into cold water while they are liquid, thus shattering the material into particles of a less troublesome size.

Studio Hints

This section may seem unnecessary to most potters, but it is included in the hope that a few suggestions may be helpful to beginning pottery students or to those working in small and expanding departments.

CLAY STORAGE can be a problem in a studio if the rather simple facilities are not available. Dry clay, which can be piled up in sacks, is easily stored. Wet clay is the culprit, since a quantity ought to be on hand at all times to age. Small quantities may be conveniently stored in plastic bags without losing moisture. Galvanized cans are the most economical solution, but they are difficult to clean and corrode after prolonged contact with wet clay. The best way to store wet clay is in large stoneware crocks which are difficult to find today. Occasionally, they can be found at reasonable prices in secondhand stores.

A SHOP LIFT on rollers with a 2-x-2-foot platform and a 6-foot vertical lift is a very handy piece of equipment in a ceramic studio. We have pallets under our large galvanized cans containing slip, scrap clay, or wash water. Thus equipped one can easily move the large cans, siphon off the water, raise them up under a wall-mounted blunger, or empty the contents into drying bats or filter tanks through a valve. Likewise stacked bagged clay may be moved conveniently. A shop lift is also a great help in moving and loading large ceramic sculptural pieces in the kiln. Kiln doors in need of repair may be removed and replaced by one person with the aid of a lift.

WASHING FACILITIES may become a minor problem in the studio since sinks are often inadequate in size or number. I always keep a large galvanized can of water near the sink. All students are required to first wash off all pans, the tools used, and their hands in this can before using the sink. In addition, all throwing or wash water is dumped here. This can not only relieves congestion at the sinks and avoids the problem of drains clogged by clay scraps but also allows for the recovery of a great deal of clay which is collected in the bottom of the can. If much throwing is done, the clay recovered may amount to as much as 100 pounds per week. When the water in the can becomes rather sliplike, it is moved by the shop lift under the blunger to break up any lump clay and then emptied through a bottom valve into a large filter tank.

A FILTER TANK may be easily improvised from a double concrete laundry tub. Hardwood slats covered by screen wire are placed about

6 inches or so below the top. This platform is covered by a heavy cloth or canvas which laps over the top edge. A surprising amount of water will drip from the slip into the tub below. At school we have reversed an old air compressor so that it functions as a vacuum. Another type of vacuum may be improvised by attaching a hose from the bottom of the tank to a running-water faucet. The special faucet fitting is constructed at an angle so that the force of the running water will create suction in the hose from the tanks. Of course, this rig does not approach the efficiency of a commercial filter press but it is a help in drying out clay slip.

WEDGING TABLES may be constructed of many materials. Some potters use a heavy cementlike slab. I prefer to use a 6-inch slab of plaster which, if needed, may be also used to dry out clay. Our best drying bats are about 2 x 3 feet and about 1 foot thick with a 5- or 6-inch hollowed-out center. In order to dry out the clay easily they are placed on an angle-iron framework. Since plaster tends to chip easily, the upper edges of the bats and wedging tables are cast with a heavy galvanized metal beading and reinforcement strips like those commonly used by plasterers for doorways instead of wood trim. Bats used for drying clay must be scraped frequently so that they will retain their absorbency. A film of soluble substances and colloidal clay is deposited on the surface of the plaster whenever it is used as a drying bat. Washing with water will not remove the film which eventually prevents the absorption of the clay moisture as effectively as a coating of varnish or wax.

ATOMIC WEIGHTS OF COMMON ELEMENTS

Element	Symbol	Atomic number	Atomic weight
Aluminum	Al	13	26.97
Antimony	Sb	51	121.76
Barium	Ba	56	137.36
Bismuth	Bi	83	209.00
Boron	B	5	10.82
Cadmium	Cd	48	112.41
Calcium	Ca	20	40.08
Carbon	C	6	12.01
Chlorine	Cl	17	35.475
Chromium	Cr	24	52.01
Cobalt	Co	27	58.94
Copper	Cu	29	63.54
Fluorine	F	9	19.00
Gold	Au	79	197.20
Helium	He	2	4.003
Hydrogen	H	1	1.008
Iridium	Ir	77	193.10
Iron	Fe	26	55.84
Lead	Pb	82	207.21
Lithium	Li	3	6.49
Magnesium	Mg	12	24.32
Manganese	Mn	25	54.93
Mercury	Hg	80	200.61
Molybdenum	Mo	42	95.95
Neon	Ne	10	20.183
Nickel	Ni	28	58.69
Nitrogen	N	7	14.008
Oxygen	O	8	16.00
Palladium	Pd	46	106.70
Phosphorus	P	15	30.98
Platinum	Pt	78	195.23
Potassium	K	19	39.096
Silicon	Si	14	28.06
Silver	Ag	47	107.88
Sodium	Na	11	22.997
Sulfur	S	16	32.066
Tin	Sn	50	118.70
Titanium	Ti	22	47.90
Uranium	U	92	238.07
Vanadium	V	23	50.95
Zinc	Zn	30	65.38
Zirconium	Zr	40	91.22

COMMON CERAMIC RAW MATERIALS

Material	Formula	Compound molecular weight	RO R_2O	R_2O_3	RO_2
Aluminum hydroxide	$Al_2(OH)_6$	156		156	
Antimony oxide	Sb_2O_3	292		292	
Barium carbonate	$BaCO_3$	197	197		
Bone ash (Calcium phosphate)	$Ca_3(PO_4)_2$	310	103		
Boric acid	$B_2O_3 \cdot 3H_2O$	124		124	
Borax	$Na_2O \cdot 2B_2O_3 \cdot 10H_2O$	382	382	191	
Calcium borate (colemanite)	$2CaO \cdot 3B_2O_3 \cdot 5H_2O$	412	206	137	
Calcium carbonate (whiting)	$CaCO_3$	100	100		
Chromium oxide	Cr_2O_3	152		152	
Cobalt carbonate	$CoCO_3$	119	119	238	
Cobalt oxide, black	Co_3O_4	241	80		
Copper carbonate	$CuCO_3$	119	119	238	
Copper oxide, green (cupric)	CuO	80	80		
Copper oxide, red (cuprous)	Cu_2O	144	72		
Cornwall stone*	$IRO \cdot 2.5Al_2O_3 \cdot 20SIO_2$	1550	1550	620	78
Cyrolite	$Na_3 \cdot AlF_6$	210	140	420	
Dolomite	$CaCO_3 \cdot MgCO_3$	184	184		
Feldspar, potash	$K_2O \cdot Al_2O_3 \cdot 6SiO_2$	557	557	557	93
Feldspar, soda	$Na_2 \cdot Al_2O_3 \cdot 6SiO_2$	524	524	524	87
Kaolin (China clay)	$Al_2O_3 \cdot 2SiO_2 \cdot 2H_2O$	258		258	129
Kaolin (calcined)	$Al_2O_3 \cdot 2SiO_2$	222		222	111
Iron chromate	$FeCrO_4$	172	172	344	
Iron oxide, red (ferric)	Fe_2O_3	160	80	160	
Iron oxide, black (ferrous)	FeO	72	72		
Flint (quartz, silica)	SiO_2	60			60
Fluorspar (calcium fluoride)	CaF_2	78	78		
Lead carbonate (white lead)	$2PbCO_3 \cdot Pb(OH)_2$	775	258		
Lead oxide (litharge)	PbO	223	223		
Lead oxide, red	Pb_3O_4	685	228		
Lepidolite	$LiF \cdot KF \cdot Al_2O_3 \cdot 3SiO_2$	356	712	356	118
Lithium carbonate	Li_2CO_3	74	74		
Magnesium carbonate	$MgCO_3$	84	84		
Manganese carbonate	$MnCO_3$	115	115		
Manganese dioxide (black)	MnO_2	87	87		
Manganese oxide (greenish)	MnO	71	71		
Nepheline syenite	$K_2O \cdot 3Na_2O \cdot 4Al_2O_3 \cdot 9SiO_2$	447	112	112	50
Nickel oxide, green	NiO	75	75		
Nickel oxide, black	Ni_2O_3	166	83		
Plastic vitrox†	$1RO \cdot 1.33Al_2O_3 \cdot 13.9SiO_2$	1051	1051	790	75
Potassium carbonate (pearl ash)	K_2CO_3	138	138		

COMMON CERAMIC RAW MATERIALS—*continued*

Material	Formula	Compound molecular weight	Equivalent Weights RO R$_2$O	R$_2$O$_3$	RO$_2$
Potassium dichromate	K$_2$Cr$_2$O$_7$	294	294		
Pyrophyllite	Al$_2$O$_3 \cdot$4SiO$_2 \cdot$H$_2$O	360		360	90
Sodium bicarbonate	NaHCO$_3$	84	168		
Sodium carbonate (soda ash)	Na$_2$CO$_3$	106	106		
Spodumene	Li$_2$O$\cdot$Al$_2$O$_3 \cdot$4SiO$_2$	372	372	372	93
Talc (steatite)	3MgO$\cdot$4SiO$_2 \cdot$H$_2$O	379	126		95
Tin oxide (stannic oxide)	SnO$_2$	151			151
Titanium dioxide (rutile impure TiO$_2$)	TiO$_2$	80			80
Zinc oxide	ZnO	81	81		
Zirconium oxide	ZnO$_2$	123			123

* Formula for Cornwall stone:

KNaO	0.63	Al$_2$O$_3$	1.3497	SiO$_2$	10.1227
CaO	0.32	Fe$_2$O$_3$	0.0181		
MgO	0.05				

† Formula for plastic vitrox:

CaO	0.053				
Na$_2$O	0.334	Al$_2$O$_3$	1.33	SiO$_2$	13.9
K$_2$O	0.613				

TEMPERATURE EQUIVALENTS
ORTON STANDARD PYROMETRIC CONES*

Cone number	Large cones		Small cones	
	150°C†	270°F†	300°C†	540°F†
020	635	1175	666	1231
019	683	1261	723	1333
018	717	1323	752	1386
017	747	1377	784	1443
016	792	1458	825	1517
015	804	1479	843	1549
014	838	1540		
013	852	1566		
012	884	1623		
011	894	1641		
010	894	1641	919	1686
09	923	1693	955	1751
08	955	1751	983	1801
07	984	1803	1008	1846
06	999	1830	1023	1873
05	1046	1915	1062	1944
04	1060	1940	1098	2008
03	1101	2014	1131	2068
02	1120	2048	1148	2098
01	1137	2079	1178	2152
1	1154	2109	1179	2154
2	1162	2124	1179	2154
3	1168	2134	1196	2185
4	1186	2167	1209	2208
5	1196	2185	1221	2230
6	1222	2232	1255	2291
7	1240	2264	1264	2307
8	1263	2305	1300	2372
9	1280	2336	1317	2403
10	1305	2381	1330	2426
11	1315	2399	1336	2437
12	1326	2419	1335	2471
13	1346	2455		
14	1366	2491		
15	1431	2608		

RAKU - *(handwritten note next to cone 014)*

* From the Edward Orton, Jr., Ceramic Foundation, Columbus 1, Ohio.

† Temperature rise per hour.

COLOR SCALE FOR TEMPERATURES

Color	Degrees centigrade	Degrees fahrenheit
Lowest visible red	475	885
Lowest visible red to dark red	475-650	885-1200
Dark red to cherry red	650-750	1200-1380
Cherry red to bright cherry red	750-815	1380-1500
Bright cherry red to orange	815-900	1500-1650
Orange to yellow	900-1090	1650-2000
Yellow to light yellow	1090-1315	2000-2400
Light yellow to white	1315-1540	2400-2800
White to dazzling white	1540 and higher	2800 and higher

AVERAGE TEMPERATURES TO WHICH VARIOUS CERAMIC PRODUCTS ARE FIRED

Products	Temperature (degree F)
Heavy clay products	
Common brick—surface clay	1600-1800
Common brick—shale	1800-2000
Face brick—shale	1950-2200
Face brick—fire clay	2100-2300
Face brick—surface clay	1750-1850
Enamel brick	2100-2300
Paving brick (vitrified)	2000-2250
Structural clay tile—surface clay	1600-1800
Structural clay tile—fire clay	1950-2100
Drain tile	1700-1900
Sewer pipe	2030-2320
Roofing tile	1960-2140
Terra cotta	2070-2320
Pottery	
Flower pots	1580-1850
Stoneware (chemical)	2650-2700
Stoneware (once fired)	2318-2426
Earthenware or semivitreous ware—bisque	2282-2354
Earthenware or semivitreous ware—glost	2174-2282
Art ware—bisque	2030-2426
Art ware—glost	1814-2426
Pottery decalcomanias	1400-1500
Refractories	
Fire brick—clay	2300-2500
Bauxite brick	2650-2800
Fire brick—silica	2650-2750
Chrome brick	2650-2800
Magnesite brick	2650-2800
Silicon carbide	3236-3992

AVERAGE TEMPERATURES TO WHICH
VARIOUS CERAMIC PRODUCTS ARE FIRED—*continued*

Products	Temperature (degree F)
Whitewares	
Electrical porcelain	2390-2500
Hotel china—bisque	2390-2436
Hotel china—glost	2210-2282
Sanitary ware—bisque	2318-2426
Sanitary ware—glost	2236-2318
Floor tile	2318-2498
Wall tile—bisque	1886-2354
Wall tile—glost	1186-2246

MELTING POINTS OF SELECTED COMPOUNDS
AND MINERALS

	Degree C		Degree F	
Alumina	2050		3722	
Barium carbonate	1360		2480	
Barium chloride	960		1760	
Barium oxide (O_2)	450	(O_2)	842	
Barium sulfate	1580		2876	
Borax	red heat			
Calcium carbonate (dissociates)	825		1517	
Calcium fluoride	1300		2372	
Calcium oxide	2570		4658	
Calcium sulfate (gypsum, dissociates)	900		1652	
Chromium oxide	1990		3614	
Cobaltic oxide (O_2)	905	(O_2)	1661	
Cobalt nitrate	56		133	
Copper oxide (Cu_2O)	1210		2210	
(CuO)	1064		1947	
Corundum	2035		3695	
Dolomite	2570-2800		4658-5072	
Dolomite (commercial)	1925-2485		3497-4505	
Ferric oxide	1548		2518	
Ferrous oxide	1419		2586	
Fire clay (high-grade)	1660-1720		3020-3128	
Fire clay (low-grade)	1600-1650		2912-3002	
Flint	1715		3119	
Fluorspar	1300		2372	
Kaolin	1740-1785		3164-3245	
Kaolinite	1785		3245	
Lead oxide (litharge)	880		1616	
Lead oxide (minimum, dissociates)	500-530		932-986	
Lime	2570		4658	
Limestone	2570		4658	
Magnesium carbonate (dissociates)	350		662	
Magnesium oxide (approx.)	2800		5072	
Manganese dioxide (O_2)	1058	(O_2)	1945	
Mullite	1810		3290	

MELTING POINTS OF SELECTED COMPOUNDS AND MINERALS—*continued*

	Degree C		Degree F
Mullite (commercial)	1790		3254
Nickel oxide (O₂)	400	(O₂)	752
Orthoclase feldspar (dissociates)	1170		2138
Potassium carbonate	880		1616
Potassium chromate	975		1787
Potassium dichromate	398		748
Potassium nitrate	337		639
Potassium oxide	red heat		
Quartz	1715		3119
Rutile	1900		3452
Rutile (commercial)	1630		2966
Silica	1715		3119
Silicon carbide (decomposed)	2200		3992
Sillimanite	1816		3301
Sillimanite (commercial)	1810		3290
Sodium carbonate	853		1567
Sodium chloride	792		1458
Sodium nitrate	313		595
Sodium oxide	red heat		
Sodium sulfate	880		1616
Spinel	2135		3875
Spinel (commercial)	1915		3479
Tin oxide	1130		2066
Titanium oxide	1900		3452
Whiting (dissociates)	825		1517
Zircon	2550		4622
Zircon (commercial)	1900-2300		3452-4172
Some glass-forming silicates			
Na_2SiO_3	1089		1992
K_2SiO_3	976		1789
$PbSiO_3$	770		1418
$BaSi_2O_5$	1426		2599

WATER OF PLASTICITY OF VARIOUS CLAYS

Crude kaolin	36.69-44.78
Washed kaolin	44.48-47.50
White sedimentary kaolin	28.60-56.25
Ball clays	25.00-53.30
Crucible clays	26.84-50.85
Refractory bond clays	32.50-37.90
Glass-pot clays	19.64-36.50
Plastic fire clays	12.90-37.40
Flint fire clays	8.89-19.04
Sagger clays	18.40-28.56
Stoneware clays	19.16-34.80
Face-brick clays	14.85-37.50
Sewer-pipe clays	11.60-36.20
Paving-brick clays	11.80-19.60
Brick clays	13.20-40.70

Glaze, Stain, and Body Recipes

Ceramic glaze formulas used to be discussed with a great deal of secrecy. Fortunately, this attitude has passed. What is done with a glaze is much more important than how it is made. The text has stressed the technical side of ceramics in order to make more studio time available for actual potting than might otherwise be possible.

Regardless of the variety of glazes and decorative devices described the student should not be too impressed by technique, however important it may be. Many of the finest potters use only a few standard glazes and stains and a minimum of decoration. Techniques are important and should be studied, but they should not overshadow the search for ideas.

The list of glazes in this section will supplement the earlier discussions of glaze types and the function of the various glaze chemicals. For convenience the glazes are listed as batch recipes. It must be stressed again that before two of these glazes can be compared with any certainty, they must be converted into empirical formula form.

Some of the glazes listed here are those used constantly in the studio. The studio glaze number is given in parenthesis. If specific colors used in the studio are desired, the student may obtain the amounts of the coloring oxides from the glaze file cards. The glazes listed here may give slightly different results depending upon the kiln, the firing schedule, and the body.

LOW-FIRE LEAD* AND ALKALINE GLAZES

Cones 05-03, Lithium Blue (N-13A)

26.9	Lithium carbonate
13.6	Kaolin
53.9	Flint
2.8	Bentonite
3.7	Copper carbonate

Cones 08-09, Chromium Red

200.6	Red lead
14.4	Potassium bichromate
6.12	Soda ash
25.8	Kaolin
54.0	Flint

Cones 04-02, Barium Mat Glaze (N-17)

20	Whiting
129	White lead
64	Potash feldspar
39	Barium carbonate
21	Calcined kaolin
37	Flint

Cones 04-02, Alumina Mat (N-12)

142.0	White lead
35.0	Whiting
63.5	Potash feldspar
40.0	Calcined kaolin
12.0	Kaolin

* In substituting red for white lead, approximately 11½% less material is needed for the same PbO.

Cone 04, Lithium Semi-opaque (from K. Green)

26.9	Lithium carbonate
25.0	White lead
12.0	Bone ash
9.0	Soda feldspar
15.6	Kaolin
53.9	Flint
2.8	Bentonite

Cone 04, Semigloss Rutile (from K. Green)

80.0	White lead
6.1	Plastic vitrox
19.0	Kaolin
16.1	Flint
7.0	Rutile

Cone 04, Semimat (N-1) (very fluid)

301.0	White lead
85.0	Potash feldspar
6.5	Kaolin
23.0	Rutile
7.5	Whiting
57.5	Borax
12.5	Calcined kaolin

Cone 04, Lead-borax Turquoise (N-4-A) fluid

47.5	Whiting
103.0	Borax
4.0	Soda ash
77.0	White lead
107.5	Potash feldspar
51.0	Flint
2.0	Kaolin
37.0	Tin oxide
13.7	Copper carbonate

Cone 04, Colemanite Crackle Glaze

102	Potash feldspar
123	Colemanite
43	Barium carbonate
33	Flint

Cone 04, Burnt-red Glaze (N-10-A)

164.0	White lead
24.5	Whiting
38.5	Kaolin
9.5	Zinc oxide
100.0	Flint
20.2	Tin oxide
13.5	Red iron oxide

Cone 04, Volcanic-ash Mat (from A. Garzio)

40	Colemanite	60	Volcanic ash
10	Whiting	35	Kaolin
5	Barium carbonate	6	Zinc oxide
12	White lead	12	Tin oxide
8	Borax		

Cone 04, Volcanic Ash (N-6)

60	Volcanic ash
20	Colemanite
10	White lead
10	Borax

MEDIUM-FIRE GLAZES, CONES 2-6

Cones 1-2, Clear Glaze

50.0	White lead
14.9	Soda feldspar
3.2	Whiting
2.7	Zinc oxide
9.4	Flint
14.8	Cornwall stone
.2	Gum tragacanth

Cone 2, Glaze

31.9	Feldspar
8.6	Whiting
26.1	Red lead
5.4	Kaolin
5.7	Ball clay
19.7	Flint

	Cone 2, Plastic Vitrox			Cone 2, Colemanite
310	White lead		24.0	Calcined zinc oxide
179	Potash feldspar		113.0	Potash feldspar
474	Plastic vitrox		51.5	Colemanite
106	Whiting		20.0	Barium carbonate
			19.0	Steatite
			66.0	Flint

	Cones 1-4, Mat		Cone 6, Semi-mat Glaze			Cone 4, Glaze
40.0	Feldspar	9.8	Whiting		15.3	Whiting
6.0	Whiting	2.1	Talc		23.0	White lead
7.5	Barium carbonate	11.0	Barium carbonate		30.0	Feldspar
6.1	Zinc oxide	4.3	Calcined zinc oxide		7.0	Kaolin
2.0	Talc	42.5	Soda feldspar		7.7	Flint
5.0	Kaolin	8.3	Kaolin			
3.8	Ball clay	8.0	Ball clay			
18.2	Flint	14.0	Flint			

PORCELAIN AND STONEWARE GLAZES, CONES 8-14

	Cone 8, Lepidolite (crackle glaze) (S-1)			Cones 8-10, Semi-mat
60	Lepidolite		66.4	Feldspar (potash)
138	Potash feldspar		8.0	Whiting
20	Cryolite		25.6	Kaolin
20	Bone ash			
40	Whiting			
40	Colemanite			

	Cones 8-10, Semi-gloss Black
100	Albany slip clay
3	Cobalt oxide, black

	Cone 8, Feldspar (S-2)			Cone 8, Semi-mat (S-3)
44.5	Soda feldspar		36.0	Potash feldspar
12.0	Whiting		25.4	Kaolin
7.3	Kaolin		17.3	Whiting
36.2	Flint		11.9	Flint
			8.1	Rutile

	Cone 8, Semi-mat Ash Glaze (S-6)			Cone 8, Crackle-ash Glaze (S-7)
40	Potash feldspar		70	Potash feldspar
40	Mixed hardwood ashes		30	Mixed hardwood ashes
20	Ball clay		10	Whiting

Cones 8-11, White Opaque

35.1	Feldspar (potash)
9.9	Kaolin (Florida)
13.5	Whiting
1.0	Borax
16.2	Flint
1.8	Zinc oxide
23.4	Zircopax

Cones 10-13, Mat (from A. Garzio)

113.5	Feldspar (potash)
35.0	Whiting
30.0	Kaolin

Cones 10-13 (from A. Garzio)

105.0	Feldspar (potash)
37.5	Whiting
37.5	Ball clay
9.0	Kaolin
6.25	Zinc oxide

Cones 10-12, Mat

38.0	Feldspar (potash)
21.0	Whiting
20.0	Kaolin
15.9	Silica
4.1	Titanium oxide

REDUCTION GLAZES

Cone 04, Celadon

154.8	White lead
12.0	Whiting
396.48	Godfrey spar (soda)
192.0	Soda ash
11.7	Red iron oxide
19.0	Tin oxide

(Grind dry, use immediately if wet. Fire: Reduction, cone 012-07; oxidizing, cone 07-04.)

Cone 04, Copper Luster

173	White lead
25	Manganese oxide
64	Cornwall stone
24	Flint
3	Copper oxide
5	Cobalt oxide

(Black when thin, copper when thick. Fire: Reduction cone 012-07; oxidizing cone 07-04.)

Cone 2, Artificial Copper-red Reduction

(from Harder)

158.0	Soda feldspar
132.0	Borax
3.5	Soda ash
31.0	Fluorspar (plus ½ of 1% silicon carbide [180 mesh carborundum])
58.0	Kaolin
83.0	Flint
8.8	Tin oxide
1.5	Copper carbonate

Cone 8, Copper-red Reduction

108.0	Cornwall stone
126.0	Flint
15.5	Zinc oxide
36.0	Barium carbonate
16.5	Soda ash
85.0	Borax
8.0	Copper carbonate
8.0	Tin oxide

Cones 6-8, Celadon Reduction

61.3	Potash feldspar
7.5	Whiting (Fire smoky to cone 012; strong reduction to cone 07; oxidizing fire to cone 6.)
4.9	Kaolin
24.8	Flint
1.5	Red iron oxide

Cone 6, Copper-red Reduction (from Curtis)

40	White lead
40	Red lead
20	Whiting
10	Kaolin
100	Flint
100	Borax
15	Boric acid
15	Soda ash
5	Tin oxide
2	Copper oxide (Fire smoky to cone 012; strong reduction to cone 07; oxidizing fire to cone 6.)

Cone 8, Artificial Reduction (S-5-A) (from Baggs)

179.0	Soda feldspar
10.6	Soda ash
152.0	Borax
40.0	Whiting
67.0	Kaolin
96.0	Flint
10.0	Tin oxide
1.6	Copper carbonate
3.5	Silicon carbide

Cones 8-10, Celadon

78	Feldspar (potash)
6	Whiting
14	Flint
2	Red iron oxide

Cones 9-10, Copper Red

13.0	Ferro Frit #3191
44.0	Feldspar (soda)
14.0	Whiting
3.0	Kaolin (Florida)
25.0	Flint
1.0	Tin oxide
0.2	Copper carbonate

(Add .2 silicon carbide for artificial reduction.)

CRYSTALLINE GLAZES

Cones 07-05, Aventurine

172.9	Borax
9.8	Borium carbonate
12.4	Boric acid
6.4	Kaolin
177.0	Flint
67.0	Red iron oxide

(Grind and use immediately or frit [without the clay].)

Cones 3-4, Aventurine

79	Ferro Frit #3304
16	Red iron oxide
5	Kaolin (Florida)

Cones 3-4, Zinc Crystal

13.1	Soda ash
15.2	Boric acid
21.7	Zinc oxide
41.8	Flint
6.6	Rutile
6.0	Ball clay

(Grind and use immediately or frit without the clay.)

Cone 8, Zinc Crystal (pale green, S-4A)

11.06	Sodium carbonate
6.28	Whiting
20.30	Zinc oxide
40.10	Silica
5.01	Titanium (rutile)
17.25	Kaolin (Florida)
3.00	Copper carbonate

(Grind and use immediately or frit [without the clay].)

Cone 11, Zinc Crystal

100	Feldspar
35	Whiting
35	Flint
50	Zinc oxide

Cone 11, Titanium Crystal

50	Soda ash
100	Flint
50	Zinc oxide
20	Titanium oxide

CERAMIC STAINS*

(For preparation, see Chapter 10)

#1 Pink Stain

50	Tin oxide
25	Whiting
18	Flint
4	Borax
3	Potassium dichromate

(Calcine to cone 8; stain is lumpy and must first be broken up in iron mortar, then ground.)

#3 Crimson Stain

22.9	Whiting
6.6	Calcium sulfate
4.4	Fluorspar
20.8	Flint
43.7	Tin oxide
1.6	Potassium dichromate

(Calcine to cone 8 and grind.)

#2 Pink Stain

50.5	Tin oxide
19.0	Whiting
7.5	Fluorspar
20.5	Flint
7.5	Potassium dichromate

(Calcine to cone 8 and grind.)

#4 Ultramarine Stain

50	Chromium oxide
12	Flint
38	Cobalt oxide (CoO, cobaltous)

(Calcine to cone 8.)

* Note: Above stains must be finely ground to obtain the desired color.

#5 Blue-green Stain

41.8	Cobalt oxide (CoO)
19.2	Chromium oxide
39.0	Aluminum oxide

(Calcine to cone 8 and grind.)

#6 Orange Stain

29.8	Antimony oxide
12.8	Tin oxide
14.9	Red iron oxide
42.5	Red lead

(Calcine to cone 6 and grind.)

#7 Black Stain

43	Chromium oxide
43	Red iron oxide
10	Manganese dioxide
4	Cobalt oxide

(Calcine to cone 8 and grind.)

#8 Turquoise Stain

56	Copper phosphate
44	Tin oxide

(Calcine to cone 6 and grind.)

#9 Red-brown Stain

22	Chromium oxide
23	Red iron oxide
55	Zinc oxide

(Calcine to cone 8 and grind.)

#10 Brown Stain

64.6	Zinc oxide
9.7	Chrome oxide
9.7	Red iron oxide
8.0	Red lead
8.0	Boric acid

(Calcine to cone 8 and grind.)

#11 Yellow Stain

33.3	Antimony oxide
50.0	Red lead
16.7	Tin oxide

(Calcine to cone 6 and grind.)

#12 Black Stain

65	Chromium oxide
35	Red iron oxide

(Calcine to cone 8 and grind.)

Clay Bodies

The body preferred by the studio potter is quite different from that used by the commercial pottery. For slip casting or jiggering a uniformity of texture is desired for obvious technical reasons. Likewise any impurities imparting color to the body are frowned upon. Therefore, bodies used in commercial production are carefully selected, ground, and refined. Plasticity is of a minor importance, and since it is associated with high shrinkage rates, it is usually avoided.

Local supplies of earthenware and plastic fire clays are available, at least in the midwest. Since they are widely used in cement, plaster, and mortar mixtures they are competitively priced and generally quite reasonable.

Since the volume of clay used in the school studio will normally run from one half a ton to two tons per year both the initial cost and shipping charges are important. Thus clay that can be obtained locally has a decided advantage even if it needs a certain amount of sieving or small additions. Occasionally a truckload of raw clay may be purchased very reasonably from a local brick or tile works.

EARTHENWARE BODIES present no real problem of supply in the Midwest since there are many brick and tile factories which also sell bagged clay. Many are shale clays with coarse particles which will cause trouble unless they are run through a sieve of from 15 to 20 meshes per inch. Some earthenware clays contain soluble sulfates which will form a whitish scum on the fired ware. Adding 1 or 2 percent barium carbonate will eliminate this fault. Many such clays will not be very plastic unless they are aged. The addition of about 5 percent of bentonite, which is extremely plastic, will usually render a short clay workable. Often two clays which alone are not suitable can be mixed together to form a good body. Only experimentation will indicate the necessary changes.

Occasionally the body will lack sufficient flint to fuse with the fluxes it contains. Cream-colored clays may be further lightened in color and rendered more plastic by the addition of ball clays. Talc has some plasticity and is often used in low-fire whiteware bodies as a source of both flux and silica. Feldspar, nepheline syenite, plastic vitrox, silica, and alumina are also added to various bodies to contribute fluxing qualities.

STONEWARE and PORCELAIN BODIES are largely compounded bodies. In fact, it is extremely rare for a single clay to satisfy all throwing and firing requirements. There is no clay which by itself will make a porcelain body. Oriental porcelain is made from one or two claylike minerals which are fairly plastic. Since nothing in the Western world compares with petuntze, porcelain bodies must be compounded from clay and various mineral compounds.

Both stoneware and porcelain will form hard vitrified bodies at cone 10. The major difference between the two is that stoneware contains various impurities, chiefly iron, which gives it a gray or tan color. Both types are compounded for varying temperatures and, in the case of porcelain, for different degrees of translucency. Greater translucency is usually obtained by increasing the silica ratio which has the accompanying defect of an increase in firing warpage.

Both fire clay and stoneware clays differ chiefly from pure clay (kaolin) in that they contain various fluxes and impurities which lower the fusion point and impart a gray, tan, or buff color. Fire clays contain a higher percentage of silica which makes it suitable for making refractory products such as kiln furniture and fire and insulating bricks.

The familiar crocks and old-fashioned jugs which we occasionally still see were made of stoneware clays. As manufacturers today desire completely white bodies, not many items are made of stoneware. Therefore, local sources of stoneware clays may not be available, or the transportation costs may be excessive. Fire clays, which have a more universal industrial use can be substituted for stoneware. Some fire clays are very plastic and fine enough for throwing purposes. They often contain some iron impurities which give the body a flecked appearance. Depending upon the temperature and appearance desired, it may be necessary to blend in an earthenware or stoneware clay or ingredients such as feldspar, talc, or silica.

The following section lists several types of clay and porcelain bodies. They are included merely as suggestions since it usually will be necessary to vary these recipes depending upon raw materials available locally.

Cone 2, Light-red Clay Body

60	Red clay
25	Flint
15	Kaolin

Cone 2, Cream Clay Body

12	Ball clay
2	Kaolin
7	Soda feldspar
5	Flint
2	Red clay

Cones 2-8, Stoneware Body

20	Jordan clay
25	Ball clay
30	Laclede fire clay
10	Nepheline syenite
5	Flint
12	Grog (fine size for wheel work)

Cones 8-10, Stoneware Body

100	Jordan
100	Fire clay
60	Grog (fine, 60-mesh)
60	Flint

Cone 8, Stoneware Body

40	Ball clay
40	Fire clay
20	Earthenware (for color and texture)

Cones 8-10, Porcelain Body

45	Kaolin
25	Feldspar (potash)
16	Ball clay
13	Flint

Cones 8-12, Porcelain Body

7	Ball clay
7	Kaolin
7	Feldspar (potash)
5	Flint

Cones 10-15, Porcelain Body

25	Ball clay
25	Kaolin
25	Feldspar (potash)
25	Flint

Sources of Materials and Equipment*

The cost of materials is an important factor in developing a ceramic program, especially if it is to be paid out of the general budget for the course. A rough estimate for the cost per student per semester is about $4 or $5, not including shipping costs which may be considerable in certain cases. The cost per student for advanced students, who produce more pottery, is, of course, greater. In addition to the cost of materials, the firing expense, which may also be charged to the department, must be considered.

All this indicates the desirability of a business-like approach to the problem of purchasing. The lower figure of $4 per student reflects the savings possible by purchasing in quantity. Supplies bought from a hobby-shop dealer, will cost a good deal more.

The cost of clay, which seems so cheap per pound, can be very deceiving. The rate at which a few classes can use up a ton of clay is really surprising. For some types of clay the shipping costs may be greater than the

* The addresses of all dealers and manufacturers listed here appear on pp. 214-215. Information on regional dealers not listed will be appreciated by the author.

cost of the clay itself. Of course, local clays can be used, but the trouble and labor of processing local clay may make this solution undesirable. Fortunately clay is commonly used in mortar and cement where, in proper amounts, it helps to provide not only a cheaper but a stronger bond. As such it is available from most building supplies dealers in 50-pound bags, usually priced from 60 to 75 cents per bag. These clays are generally shale earthenware which needs sieving. Often bentonite or flint or talc are necessary to make it suitable. But even then these clays represent considerable savings. In a similar manner, many fire clays can be procured from local dealers where they are normally sold for repairing furnaces and industrial ovens. With a little doctoring these fire clays,

which are often quite plastic, can be converted into satisfactory stoneware bodies.

Coloring oxides, which are used in small amounts can be purchased in small quantities. Even a small department, however, should purchase the more common chemicals like lead, flint, borax, or the feldspars, in 100-pound lots. These may not be used up for several years but the savings in purchasing the larger quantity are so great that the greater purchase is warranted.

In ordering it is occasionally advisable to buy in a few bulky but cheap items so that the shipment will not have to travel at the expensive parcel-post rate but can be sent instead by freight or motor truck.

SUPPLY DEALERS

EAST COAST

Clays

O. W. Ketcham Architectural Tile Co.
Langley Ceramic Studio
Mandl Ceramic Supply Co.
Newton Pottery Supply Co.
Pottery Arts Supply Co.
Roder Ceramic Studio
Rowantree Pottery
Stewart Clay Co.
United Clay Mines
Jack D. Wolfe, Inc.
Local building-supplies dealers

Kilns

W. H. Fairchild (electric)
L. & L. Manufacturing Co. (electric)
Roder Ceramic Studio (electric)
Unique Kilns (gas and electric)

Miscellaneous Equipment†

Craftools, Inc.
B. F. Drakenfeld, Inc.
O. Hommel Co.
Roder Ceramic Studio

Pug Mills*

Chambers Brothers Co.
Crossley Machine Co.

Ceramic Chemicals

Ceramic Color and Chemical Manufacturing Co.
Gare Ceramic Supply Co.
O. Hommel Co.
Langley Ceramic Studio
Newton Pottery Supply Co.
Vitro Manufacturing Co.
Whittaker, Clack and Daniels, Inc.
Jack D. Wolfe, Inc.

† These dealers carry spray guns, ball mills, mortars, and so forth.
* Suppliers of pug mills also carry filter presses, blungers, and so forth.

*Frits**

Pemco Corp.
Vitro Manufacturing Co.

Potter's Wheels

Craftools, Inc. (kick and electric)
Crossley Machine Co. (industrial)
Randall Wheel (kick)

Insulating Materials

Armstrong Cork Co.
Babcock and Wilcox Co.
Johns-Manville Co.

Used Equipment

Hermer Kleiner
Perry Equipment Supply Co.

MIDWEST AND SOUTH

Clays

Cedar Heights Clay Co.
Christy Firebrick Co.
Croxall Chemical and Supply Co.
General Refractories Co.
Donald Hagar
V. R. Hood, Jr.
Illinois Clay Products Co.
Kentucky-Tennessee Clay Co.
La Mo Refractory Supply Co.
Trinity Ceramic Supply Co.
Western Stoneware Co.
Zanesville Stoneware Co.
Local building supplies dealers

Kilns

J. T. Abernathy (electric and gas)
Allied Engineering Corp. (gas)
American Art Clay Co. (electric)
Harrop Ceramic Service Co. (electric)
Paragon Industries, Inc. (electric)

Ceramic Chemicals

Croxall Chemical and Supply Co.
George Fetzer

* Clear glazes.

Harshaw Chemical Co.
Illini Ceramic Service
Kraft Chemical Co.
Trinity Ceramic Supply Co.

*Frits**

Ferro Corp.
Harshaw Chemical Co.

Potter's Wheels

J. T. Abernathy (kick and electric)
American Art Clay Co. (kick and electric)
H. Littleton (kick)
H. B. Klopfenstein & Sons (kick)

Miscellaneous Equipment

American Art Clay Co.
Binks Manufacturing Co. (spray equipment)
De Vilbiss Co. (spray equipment)
Tepping Ceramic Supply Co.
U.S. Stoneware Co. (ball mills)

Pug Mills

International Clay Machinery Co.
Mixing Equipment Co. (blungers)
The Stevenson Co.
St. Paul Pug Mill

Insulating Materials

A. P. Green Fire Brick Co.
Illinois Clay Products Co.
Johns-Manville Corp.
La Mo Refractory Supply Co.

WEST AND PACIFIC COAST

Clays

L. H. Butcher Co.
Cannon Co.
Denver Fire Clay Co.
Garden City Clay Co.
Gladding, McBean & Co.

Van Howe Co.
S. Paul Ward, Inc.
Western Ceramic Supply Co.
Westwood Ceramic Supply Co.

Kilns

Advanced Kiln Co. (gas)
A. D. Alpine, Inc. (gas)
Denver Fire Clay Co. (gas and oil)
Dickinson Kilns, Inc. (gas and electric)

Ceramic Chemicals

L. H. Butcher Co.
Van Howe Co.
S. Paul Ward, Inc.
Western Ceramic Supply Co.
Westwood Ceramic Supply Co.

Potter's Wheels

Advanced Kiln Co. (electric)
A. D. Alpine, Inc. (electric)
Denver Fire Clay Co. (electric)
Skutt & Son (electric)
Paul Soldner (kick)

Miscellaneous Equipment

L. H. Butcher Co.
Van Howe Co.
S. Paul Ward, Inc.
Westwood Ceramic Supply Co.

Pug Mills

Fernholtz Machinery Co.
C. O. Fiedler Inc.

ADDRESSES OF LISTED DEALERS

Abernathy, J. T., Ceramic Studio, 212 S. State St., Ann Arbor, Mich.

Advanced Kiln Co., 944 East Slauson Ave., Los Angeles 11, Calif.

Allied Engineering Corp. (division of Ferro Corp.), 4150 East 56th St., Cleveland 5, Ohio

Alpine, A. D., Inc., 11837 Teale St., Culver City, Calif.

American Art Clay Co., 4717 West 16th St., Indianapolis 24, Ind.

Armstrong Cork Co., Lancaster, Pa.

Babcock and Wilcox Co., 161 East 42nd St., New York 17, N.Y.

Binks Manufacturing Co., 3128 Carroll Ave., Chicago 12, Ill.

Butcher, L. H., Co., 15th and Vermont Sts., San Francisco, Calif.

Cannon & Co., Box 802, Sacramento, Calif.

Cedar Heights Clay Co., 50 Portsmouth Rd., Oak Hill, Ohio

Chambers Brothers Co., 52nd St. cor. Media, Philadelphia 31, Pa.

Ceramic Color and Chemical Manufacturing Co., P.O. Box 81, New Brighton, Pa.

Christy Firebrick Co., 506 Oliver St., St. Louis 1, Mo.

Craftools, Inc., 401 Broadway, New York 13, N.Y.

Crossley Machine Co., 301 Monmouth St., Trenton 9, N.J.

Croxhall Chemical and Supply Co., P.O. Box 757, East Liverpool, Ohio

Denver Fire Clay Co., 3033 Black St., Denver 17, Colo.

De Vilbiss Co., 300 Phillips Ave., Toledo 1, Ohio

Dickinson Kilns, Inc., 2424 Glover Pl., Los Angeles 31, Calif.

Drakenfeld, B. F., Inc., 45 Park Pl., New York 7, N.Y.

Fairchild, W. H., 712 Centre St., Freeland, Pa.

Fernholtz Machinery Co., 8468 Melrose Pl., Los Angeles 46, Calif.

Ferro Corp., 4150 East 56th St., Cleveland 5, Ohio

Fetzer, George, 1205 17th Ave., Columbus 11, Ohio

Fiedler, C. O., Inc., 2221 East 37th St., Los Angeles 58, Calif.

Garden City Clay Co., Redwood City, Calif.

Gare Ceramic Supply Co., 165 Rosemont St., Haverhill, Mass.

General Refractories Co., 7640 Chicago Ave., Detroit 4, Mich.

Gladding, McBean & Co., Lincoln, Calif.

Green, A. P., Fire Brick Co., Mexico, Mo.

Hager, Donald, representative for Cooley Clay Co., Zanesville, Ohio

Hommel, O., Co., 209 4th Ave., Pittsburgh 30, Pa.

Hood, V. R., Jr., Box 1213, San Antonio 6, Tex.

Illini Ceramic Service, 439 North Wells Street, Chicago 10, Ill.

Illinois Clay Products Co., Barber Bldg., Joliet, Ill.

International Clay Machinery Co., 1145 Bolander St., Dayton 1, Ohio

Johns-Manville Co., 22 East 40th St., New York 16, N.Y.

Kentucky-Tennessee Clay Co., Mayfield, Ohio

Ketcham, O. W., Architectural Tile Co., 125 North 18th St., Philadelphia, Pa.

Kleiner, Herman, Creektown Pottery, Mount Holly, N.J.

Klopfenstein, H. B., & Sons, Route 2, Crestline, Ohio

Kraft Chemical Co., 917 West 18th St., Chicago 8, Ill.

L & L Manufacturing Co., Chester 11, Pa.

La Mo Refractory Supply Co., 323 Iris Ave., New Orleans 21, La.

Langley Ceramic Studio, 413 South 24th St., Philadelphia, Pa.

Littleton, H., Route 1, Verona, Wis.

Mandl Ceramic Supply Co., 35 Fogarty Dr., Trenton 9, N.J.

Mixing Equipment Co., 135 Mt. Read Blvd., Rochester 3, N.Y.

Newton Potters Supply Co., 1021 Boylston St., Newton 61, Mass.

Paragon Industries, Inc., Box 10133, Dallas 7, Tex.

Pemco Corp., 5601 Eastern Ave., Baltimore 24, Md.

Perry Equipment Supply Co., 1421 North 6th St., Philadelphia, Pa.

Pottery Arts Supply Co., 2554 Greenmount Ave., Baltimore 18, Md.

Randall Wheel, Box 531, Alfred, N.Y.

Roder Ceramic Studio, 500 Broadway, Clifton Heights, Pa.

Rowantree Pottery, Blue Hill, Me.

St. Paul Pug Mill, c/o Joe Kolb, North St. Paul Welding, 2524 Gene St., St. Paul, Minn.

Skutt & Son, Box 202, Olympia, Wash.

Soldner, Paul, 225 East 11th St., Claremont, Calif.

Stevenson Co., The, Wellsville, Ohio

Stewart Clay Co., 133 Mulberry St., New York, N.Y.

Tepping Ceramic Supply Co., 3517 Riverside Dr., Dayton, Ohio

Trinity Ceramic Supply Co., 9016 Diplomacy Row, Dallas 35, Tex.

Unique Kilns, 530 Spruce St., Trenton, N.J.

United Clay Mines Corp., Trenton 6, N.J.

U.S. Stoneware Co., Akron 9, Ohio.

Van Howe Co., 1185 South Cherokee Ave., Denver, Colo.

Vitro Manufacturing Co., 60 Greenway Dr., Pittsburgh 4, Pa.

Ward, S. Paul, Inc., 60 Mission St., South Pasadena, Calif.

Western Ceramic Supply Co., 1601 Howard St., San Francisco, Calif.

Western Stoneware Co., Monmouth, Ill.

Westwood Ceramic Supply Co., 610 Venice Blvd., Venice, Calif.

Whittaker, Clarke and Daniels, Inc., 260 West Broadway, New York 13, N.Y.

Wolfe, Jack D., Co., Inc., 724–734 Meeker Ave., Brooklyn 22, N. Y.

Zanesville Stoneware Co., Zanesville, Ohio

References

REFERENCES FOR THE STUDENT POTTER

Binns, Charles, *The Potter's Craft*, 3d ed. New York: Van Nostrand, 1947. The text is of a general nature and is intended for the beginning student. Mr. Binns is well known for his research work on glazes.

Kenny, John B., *The Complete Book of Pottery Making*. Philadelphia: Chilton, 1949. A good text for the beginning student, this book is clearly written and has many excellent illustrations of forming techniques.

Leach, Bernard, *A Potter's Book*. Hollywood-by-the-Sea, Fla.: Transatlantic Arts, 1951. Mr. Leach, perhaps the best-known independent studio potter today, has written an extremely readable book, and from the creative point of view, it cannot be recommended too highly. Illustrated.

Norton, F. H., *Ceramics for the Artist Potter*. Reading, Mass.: Addison-Wesley, 1956. Mr. Norton covers the entire range of ceramics from the forming processes to the chemistry of glazes, with numerous illustrations. A recommended text.

Wildenhain, Marguerite, *Pottery: Form and Expression*. New York: American Craftsmen's Council, 1959. This beautifully illustrated book by one of America's foremost potters has a moving expression of the art of living as well as the art of ceramics.

SUPPLEMENTAL TEXTS

Eley, Vincent, *A Monk at the Potter's Wheel*. Leicester, Eng.: Ward, 1952. This interesting account of a young monk who decided to start a pottery at his monastery also contains some very practical information.

Home, Ruth M., *Ceramics for the Potter*. Peoria, Ill.: Bennett, 1953. This volume contains some very useful information on clays and glazes from both the historical and contemporary viewpoints. There is also a section on native Canadian clays.

HISTORICAL BACKGROUND

Cox, Warren E., *The Book of Pottery and Porcelain*, 2 vols. New York: Crown, 1944. While Mr. Cox's book is not very detailed, it is an adequate survey of the ceramic arts of all ages with many illustrations.

REFERENCES FOR THE ADVANCED POTTER

Andrews, A. T., *Ceramic Tests and Calculations*. New York: Wiley, 1928. A standard text for ceramic glaze, clay, and frit calculations.

Hetherington, A. L., *Chinese Ceramic Glazes*. Los Angeles: Commonwealth Press, 1948. A small, very readable volume, dealing primarily with Sung iron and copper glazes.

Koenig, J. H., and W. H. Earhart, *Literature Abstracts of Ceramic Glazes*. Ellenton, Fla.: College Institute, 1951. Condensations with formulas of all important articles on glazes appearing in American trade magazines, Ceramic Society publications, and British, German, and other foreign publications.

Norton, F. H., *Elements of Ceramics*. Reading, Mass.: Addison-Wesley, 1952. An introductory text for ceramic engineers, containing technical information on minerals, clays, and glazes, and on various commercial refining and production processes.

Parmelee, Cullen W., *Ceramic Glazes*. Chicago: Industrial Publications, 1951. A very complete and comprehensive text on ceramic glaze materials, slips, glazes, chemical reactions, and glaze calculations.

Rhodes, Daniel, *Clay and Glazes for the Potter*. Philadelphia: Chilton, 1957. An extremely clear treatment of clays, glazes, and calculations. A recommended text.

——, *Stoneware and Porcelain*. Philadelphia: Chilton, 1959. A companion book to *Clay and Glazes for the Potter*. In addition to a discussion of stoneware and porcelain, the book contains a great deal of useful studio information, including a chapter on kilns. A recommended text.

Rosenthal, Ernst, *Pottery and Ceramics*. Harmondsworth, Middlesex, Eng.: Pelican, 1949. A complete survey of the ceramic field, primarily from an industrial viewpoint.

Searle, A. B., *The Glazer's Book*. London: The Technical Press, 1948. A small, clearly written text on ceramic chemicals, glazes, and calculations.

MAGAZINES AND PROFESSIONAL JOURNALS

Ceramic Age, 9 Chester Bldg., Cleveland 14, Ohio. An industrial magazine of little interest to the studio potter.

Ceramic Data Book, Industrial Publications, 5 S. Wabash Ave., Chicago 3, Ill. Published annually, covering supplies and manufacturers of ceramic equipment.

Ceramic Industry, 5 S. Wabash Ave., Chicago 3, Ill. Like *Ceramic Age*, an industrial trade magazine.

Ceramic Monthly, 4175 N. High St., Columbus 14, Ohio. Oriented toward the hobby potter; many useful articles.

Craft Horizons, 29 West 53rd St., New York 19, N.Y. Covering all craft fields, with numerous articles on contemporary American and foreign ceramics; well illustrated; highly recommended.

Journal of the American Ceramic Society, Columbus, Ohio. Technical articles, usually of an industrial nature but occasionally of interest to the studio potter.

FOREIGN PUBLICATIONS

Crafts Review, Pendley Manor, Tring, Herts, Eng. A well-illustrated review covering the entire crafts field; not limited to English work.

Dansk Kunstaandvaerk, Palaegade 4, Copenhagen, Den. Covers the entire Danish design field, well illustrated; many sections are in English.

Domus, Via Monte di Pieta 15, Milan, Italy. Covers the decorative arts fields, emphasizing architecture; beautifully illustrated.

Form, Svenska Slöjdföreningen, Nybrogatan 7, Stockholm, Sweden. This journal of the Swedish Design Society covers all design fields; well illustrated. Contains a short English section.

Pottery Quarterly, Pendley Manor, Tring, Herts, Eng. Edited by a practicing potter, the *Quarterly*, unlike American magazines in the field, has a more philosophical approach. Illustrated.

GLOSSARY
OF CERAMIC TERMS

No attempt has been made to develop an elaborate glossary. For the most part, the terms included here are only those which have a meaning peculiar to the ceramic field. See also Chapter 9.

absorbency The ability of a material (clay, plaster of Paris, and so forth) to soak up water.

acid One of three types of chemicals which constitute a glaze, the other two being the bases and the intermediates or neutrals. The acid group is symbolized by the radical RO_2. The most important acid is silica (SiO_2).

Albany slip A natural clay containing sufficient fluxes to melt and function as a glaze. It develops a dark brown-black glaze at cone 8-10 without any additions. Since it is mined in several localities in the vicinity of Albany, New York, its composition may vary slightly from time to time. Similar clays, found in various sections of the country, were much used by early American stoneware potteries.

alumina (Al_2O_3) A major ingredient found in all clays and glazes. It is the chief oxide in the neutral group (R_2O_3) and imparts greater strength and higher firing temperatures to the body and glaze. When added to a glaze, it will assist in the formation of mat textures.

ash Generally, the ashes of trees, straw, leaves, and so forth. It is commonly used in the Far East to provide from 40 to 60 percent of high-temperature glaze ingredients. Depending upon the type, it will contain from 40 to 75 percent silica, from 5 to 15 percent alumina, and smaller amounts of iron, phosphorus, lime, potash, and magnesia.

alkali Generally, the base compounds of sodium and potassium but also the alkaline earth compounds, lime and magnesia. They function as fluxes, combining easily with silica.

aventurine A glaze composed of a soda, lead, or boric oxide flux with often an excess of iron oxide (over 6 percent). If it is cooled slowly, iron crystals will form and these crystals will sparkle and glisten beneath the surface of the glaze.

ball clay An extremely fine-grained, plastic, sedimentary clay. Although ball clay contains considerable organic matter, it fires out white or near white in color. It is usually added to porcelain and whiteware bodies to increase plasticity.

ball mill A porcelain jar filled with flint pebbles and rotated with either a wet or dry charge of chemicals. It is used to blend and to grind glaze and body ingredients.

barium carbonate ($BaCO_3$) Used in combination with other fluxes to form mats in the low-temperature range. A very small percentage (1 to 3) added to a clay body will prevent discoloration caused by soluble sulphates, such as the whitish blotches often seen on red bricks and earthenware bodies in general.

basalt ware A hard, black, unglazed stoneware body developed about 1775 by the Wedgwood potteries in England in an effort to imitate classical wares.

bat A disk or slab of plaster of Paris on which pottery is formed or dried. It is also used to remove excess moisture from plastic clay.

batch Raw chemicals comprising a ceramic glaze which have been weighed out in a specific proportion designed to melt at a predetermined temperature.

bentonite An extremely plastic clay formed by decomposed volcanic ash and glass which is used to render short clays workable and to aid glaze suspension.

biscuit or **bisque** Unglazed low-fired ware.

bisque fire Preliminary firing (about cone 010) prior to glazing and subsequent firing at a higher temperature.

blowing The bursting of pots in a kiln caused by a too-rapid temperature rise. The water content of the clay turns into steam and forces the body to expand and explode.

blunger A mixing machine with revolving paddles used to prepare large quantities of clay slip.

bone china A hard translucent chinaware produced chiefly in England. The body contains a large amount of bone ash (calcium phosphate) which allows it to mature at cone 10 (2380°F). It is not very plastic and therefore difficult to form; it also tends to warp.

calcine To heat a ceramic material or mixture to the temperature necessary to drive off the chemical water, carbon dioxide, and other volatile gases. Some fusion may occur in which case the material must be ground. This is the process used in the production of plaster of Paris, Portland cement, ceramic stains, and so forth.

casting (or Slip Casting) A reproductive process of forming clay objects by pouring a clay slip into a hollow plaster mold and allowing it to remain long enough for a layer of clay to thicken on the mold wall. After hardening, the clay object is removed.

chemical water Water (H_2O) chemically combined in the glaze and body compounds. At approximately 450°C (842°F) during the firing cycle this water will begin to leave the body and glaze as water vapor. Little shrinkage occurs at this point although there is a loss in weight.

china clay *See* **kaolin.**

china A loosely applied term referring to whiteware bodies fired at low porcelain temperatures. They are generally vitreous, with an absorbency of less than 2 percent, and may be translucent.

clay Basically, a decomposed granite-type rock. To be classed as a clay the decomposed rock must have fine particles so that it will be plastic. Clays should be free of vegetable matter but will often contain other impurities which affect their color and firing temperatures. They are classified into various types, such as ball clays, fire clays, and slip clays. Pure clay chemically is $Al_2O_3 \cdot 2SIO_2 \cdot 2H_2O$.

coefficient of expansion The ratio of change between the length of a material mass and the temperature.

coiling A hand method of forming pottery by building up the walls with ropelike rolls of clay and then smoothing over the joints.

combing A method of decoration developed by dragging a coarse comb or tool over two contrasting layers of wet clay slip or glaze.

Cornwall stone (also Cornish stone) A feldsparlike material found in England and widely used there for porcelain-type bodies and glazes. Compared to American feldspar, it contains more silica and a smaller amount, though a greater variety, of fluxes. It comes closest to approximating the Chinese *petuntze*, which is a major ingredient of Orient porcelain bodies and glazes.

crackle glaze A glaze containing minute cracks in the surface. The cracks are decoration and often accentuated by coloring matter that is rubbed in. They are caused by the different rates at which the body and glaze cool and contract after firing.

crawling A glaze defect generally caused by an excessive application of glaze which cracks upon drying. In the firing these cracks do not fuse but tend to separate further, exposing the clay body.

crazing An undesirable and excessive crackle in the glaze which penetrates through the glaze to the clay body. It should be remedied by adjusting the glaze or body composition to obtain a more uniform cooling and contraction rate.

crystal glazes Glazes characterized by crystalline clusters of various shapes and colors embedded in a more uniform and opaque glaze. The crystals are larger than in aventurine and may on occasion cover the entire surface. The glaze ingredients generally used are iron, lime, zinc, or rutile with an alkaline flux. A slow cooling cycle is also necessary for the development of the crystals.

cupric and **cuprous oxides** Copper oxides (CuO, Cu_2O), the major green colorants. They will also produce red under reducing conditions.

damp box A lined metal cabinet in which unfinished clay objects are stored to prevent them from drying out.

delft ware A light-colored pottery body covered with a lead-tin glaze with overglaze decorations in cobalt on the unfired glaze. Delft was first made in Holland in imitation of Chinese blue and white porcelain.

deflocculant Sodium carbonate or sodium silicate used in a casting slip to reduce the amount of water necessary and to maintain a better suspension.

della Robbia ware Ceramic sculpture of glazed terra cotta, generally in relief, produced in Florence by Lucca della Robbia or his family during the fifteenth century. The glaze used was the lead-tin majolica type developed in Spain. The modeling and the glazing were unique and established a new dimension and direction for ceramic sculpture. The early pieces were generally glazed a creamy white with a soft blue background. Later works of the workshop tended to become more colorful and less sculptural.

dipping Glazing pottery by immersing it in a large pan or vat of glaze.

dryfoot To clean the bottom of a glazed piece before firing.

dunting Crackling of fired ware in a cooling kiln—the result of opening the flues and cooling too rapidly.

earthenware Low - fired pottery (under 2000°F), usually red or tan in color with an absorbency of from 5 to 20 percent.

eggshell porcelain Translucent, thin-walled porcelain ware.

empirical formula Generally a glaze formula expressed in molecular proportions.

engobe A claylike slip which is applied to a raw or bisque body either to change the color or to give a harder and smoother surface. It may contain fluxes, silica, and so forth to adjust shrinkages.

equivalent weight A weight which will yield one unit of a component (RO or R_2O_3 or RO_2 in a compound. This is usually the same as the molecular weight of the chemical compound in question. In ceramic calculations, equivalent weights are also assigned to the RO, R_2O_3, and the RO_2 oxide groups which make up the compound. If one of these oxide groups contains more than one unit of the oxide, its equivalent weight would be found by dividing the compound molecular weight by this unit number. (See Chapter 9.)

faïence Earthenware covered with a lead-tin glaze. The French term for earthenware from the Italian pottery center at Faenza, which during the Renaissance produced this ware partially in imitation of Spanish majolica ware. *See also* **majolica** and **delft ware.**

fat clay A plastic clay such as ball clay.

ferric and **ferrous oxides** (Fe_2O_3 and FeO) Red and black iron oxides. As impurities in clay they lower the firing temperature. They are the chief source of tan and brown ceramic colors and, under reducing conditions, the various celadon greens. *See* **reduction.**

fire box Combustion chamber of a gas, oil, or wood-fired kiln, usually directly below the kiln chamber.

fire clay A clay having a slightly higher percentage of fluxes than pure clay (kaolin). It fires tan or gray in color and is used in the manufacture of refractory materials, such as bricks, muffles, and so forth for industrial glass and steel furnaces. It is often quite plastic and may be used by the studio potter as an ingredient of stoneware-type bodies.

flues Passageways around the kiln chamber through which the heating gases pass from the fire box to the chimney.

flux Lowest-melting compound in a glaze such as lead, borax, soda ash, or lime and including the potash or soda contained in the feldspars. The flux combines easily with silica and thereby helps break the higher-melting alumina-silica compounds eventually to form a glass.

foot The ringlike base of a ceramic piece, usually heavier than the surrounding body.

frit A partial or complete glaze which is melted and then reground for the purpose of eliminating the toxic effects of lead or the solubility of borax, soda ash, and so forth.

frit china A glossy, partly translucent chinaware produced by adding a glass frit to the body.

galena Lead sulphite, used as a flux for earthenware glazes, more common in Europe than in the United States.

glaze A liquid suspension of finely ground minerals which is applied by brushing, pouring, or spraying on the surface of bisque-fired ceramic ware. After drying the ware is fired to the temperature at which the glaze ingredients will melt together to form a glassy surface coating.

glaze fire A firing cycle to the temperature at which the glaze materials will melt to form a glasslike surface coating. This is usually at the point of maximum body maturity and it is considerably higher than the first bisque fire.

globar A patented carborundum-type material used in the form of rods for elements in electric kilns firing at temperatures up to cone 18. Such kilns must be used with a special transformer.

glost fire A glaze firing which is at a lower temperature than the bisque fire, usually employed only with thin chinaware which warps badly at high temperatures. In this case the bisque ware has previously been fired to its maximum body temperature. To prevent warping in the high bisque fire, the ware is placed upside down on its rim or with protective disks on the lips. Some pieces may be embedded in a layer of flint sand.

greenware Pottery which has not been bisque fired.

grog Hard fired clay which has been crushed or ground to various particle sizes. It is used to reduce shrinkage in such ceramic products as sculpture and architectural terra-cotta tiles, which, because of their thickness, have drying and shrinkage problems. From 20 to 40 percent grog may be used depending upon the amount of detail desired and whether the pieces are free standing or pressed in molds.

gum arabic or **gum tragacanth** Natural gums used as binders to enable the glaze to adhere better to the body. Binders are necessary for fritted glazes containing little or no raw clay. They are also useful when a bisque fire accidentally goes too high, or in reglazing. The gum, of course, burns completely out during the firing.

hard paste True porcelain which is fired to cone 12 or above (2420°F); also called *hard porcelain.*

ilmenite ($TiO_2 \cdot FeO$) An important source of titanium. In the granular form it is used to give dark flecks to the glaze. It is often sprinkled upon the wet glaze without previous mixing.

iron oxide *See* **ferric oxide.**

jiggering An industrial method of producing pottery. A slab of soft clay is placed upon a revolving plaster bat shaped in the negative of the object to be formed. As the wheel head turns, a metal template on a moving arm trims off the excess clay and forms the bottom, or the reverse side.

jollying A method similar to jiggering but used to produce hollow ware, such as cups.

kanthal A special metal alloy produced in Sweden for wire or strip elements in electric kilns firing from 2000° to 2400°F.

kaolin ($Al_2O_3 \cdot 2SiO_2 \cdot 2H_2O$) Pure clay, also known as china clay. It is used in glaze and porcelain bodies and fires out to a pure white. Sedimentary kaolins found in Florida are more plastic than the residual types found in the Carolinas and Georgia.

kiln A furnace made of refractory clay materials for firing ceramic products.

kiln furniture Refractory shelves and posts upon which ceramic ware is placed while being fired in the kiln.

kiln wash A protective coating of refractory materials applied to the surface of the shelves and the kiln floor to prevent excess glaze from fusing the ware tight. An inexpensive and effective wash may be made from equal parts of flint and kaolin.

kneading Working clay with the fingers or with the heel of the hand in order to obtain a uniform consistency.

lead White lead (basic lead carbonate, $2PbCo_3 \cdot Pb(OH)_2$), red lead (Pb_3O_4), and galena (lead sulphide, PbS) are among the most common low-fired fluxes.

leather hard The condition of the raw ware when most of the moisture has left the body but when it is still soft enough to be carved or burnished easily.

limestone A major flux in the medium- and high-fire temperature ranges when it is powdered in the form of whiting (calcium carbonate). If a coarse sand is used as a grog, it should not contain limestone particles. Calcined lime will expand in the bisque and cause portions of the body to pop out.

luster A type of metallic decoration thought to have been discovered in Egypt and further developed in Persia during the ninth and fourteenth centuries. A mixture of a metallic salt, resin, and bismuth nitrate is applied over a glazed piece and then refired at a lower temperature. The temperature, however, must be sufficient to melt the metal which leaves a thin layer of metal on the decorated portions.

luting A method of joining together two pieces of dry or leather-hard clay with a slip.

majolica Earthenware covered with a soft tin-bearing glaze, often with a luster decoration. The ware originally came from Spain and derived its name from the island of Majorca which lay on the trade route to Italy. Faenza ware was greatly influenced by these Spanish imports. All Renaissance pottery of this type is now generally called majolica ware.

mat glaze A dull-surfaced glaze with no gloss but pleasant to the touch, not to be confused with an incompletely fired glaze. Mat surfaces may be developed by the addition of barium carbonate, or alumina, and a slow cooling cycle.

maturity The temperature or time at which a clay or clay body develops the desirable characteristics of maximum nonporosity and hardness; or the point at which the glaze ingredients enter into complete fusion, developing a strong bond with the body, a stable structure, maximum resistance to abrasion, and a pleasant surface texture.

molds A form or box, usually made of

plaster of Paris, containing a hollow negative shape. The positive form is made by pouring either wet plaster or slip into this hollow. *See* **casting.**

muffle A lining, made of refractory materials, inside the kiln chamber and around which the hot gases pass from the fire box to the chimney. The purpose is to protect the ware from the direct flames of the fire and the resulting combustion impurities. Some of these panels are removed for a reduction fire.

muffle kiln A kiln with muffle features in contrast to a kiln using saggars. *See* **saggars.**

mullite Interlocking needlelike crystals of aluminum silicate $(3Al_2O_3 \cdot 2SiO_2)$ which form in high-temperature bodies between 1850° to 2200°F. This formation is responsible for much of the greater toughness and hardness of stoneware and porcelain, and in particular for the closer union developed between the glaze and the body.

neutral fire A fire which is neither oxidizing nor reducing. Actually this can only be obtained in practice by a slight alternation between oxidation and reduction.

opacifier A chemical whose crystals are relatively insoluble in the glaze, thereby preventing the light from penetrating the glass formation. The color most sought after is white although for some purposes others may be as effective. Tin oxide is by far the best opacifier. Zirconium, titanium, and zinc oxides are also used. Many other oxides are effective in certain combinations and within limited firing ranges. These are commercially available in frit forms under trade names, such as Zircopax and Opax.

overglaze Decoration applied with overglaze colors, either on the raw glaze or on the glazed and fired ware. In the latter case, the firing of the overglazed ware is at a lower temperature than the glaze fire.

overglaze colors Colors containing coloring oxides or ceramic stains, a flux, and some type of siccative. The fluxes are necessary to allow the colors to melt into the harder glaze to which they are applied. The lower temperatures at which most underglazes are fired (about cone 016-013) allow the use of colorants which are unstable at higher temperatures.

oxidizing fire A fire during which the kiln chamber retains an ample supply of oxygen. This means that the combustion in the fire box must be perfectly adjusted. An electric kiln always gives an oxidizing fire.

paste The compounded bodies of European-type porcelains.

peach bloom A copper-red reduction glaze with a peachlike pink color (Chinese).

peeling Separation of the glaze or slip from the body. Peeling may be caused when slip is applied to a body which is too dry, or when a glaze is applied too thickly or to a dusty surface.

peep hole A hole placed in either the fire box, kiln chamber, or muffle flues of a kiln through which one can observe the cones or the process of combustion.

petuntze A partially decomposed feldspar-type rock found in China, roughly similar in composition to Cornwall stone. With kaolin it forms the body of Oriental porcelains.

plaster of Paris Hydrate of calcium sulphate, made by calcining gypsum. It hardens after being mixed with water. Because it absorbs moisture and it can be cut and shaped easily, it is used in ceramics for drying and throwing bats, as well as for molds and casting work.

plasticity The quality of clay which allows it to be manipulated and still maintain its shape without cracking or sagging.

porcelain (Chinese) A hard, nonabsorbent clay body, white or gray in color, which rings when struck.

porcelain (hard) A hard, nonabsorbent clay body which is white and translucent.

In both types of hard porcelain the bisque is low fired and the glaze is very high (generally cone 14-16 and as high as cones 18-20 for Copenhagen porcelains).

pottery Earthenware; a shop in which ceramic objects are made.

pressing Forming of clay objects by pressing soft clay between two plaster molds, such as in the production of cup handles.

pug mill A machine for mixing plastic clay.

pyrometer An instrument for measuring heat at high temperatures. It consists of a calibrated dial connected to wires made of two different alloys, the welded tips of which protrude into the kiln chamber. When heated, these tips set up a minute electrical current which registers on the indicating dial.

pyrometric cones Small triangular cones ($1\frac{1}{8}$ and $2\frac{5}{8}$ inches in height) made of ceramic materials which are compounded to bend and melt at specific temperatures, thus enabling the potter to determine when the firing is complete.

quartz Flint or silica (SiO_2).

raku A soft, lead-glazed, hand-built groggy earthenware made in Japan and associated with the tea ceremony.

reducing agent Material in a glaze or a body, such as silicon carbide, which gives off carbon monoxide during the firing.

reduction fire A fire in which combustion is incomplete and no oxygen remains in the kiln chamber, thus causing the metallic coloring oxides in the glaze and body to lose oxygen and to revert to their metallic forms. Moth balls or pine splinters inserted in the peep hole of the chamber will cause a similar effect. Reduction is the method of producing copper reds and celadons.

refractory The quality of resisting the effects of high temperatures; also materials, high in alumina and silica, that are used for making kiln insulation, muffles, and kiln furniture.

rib A tool of wood, bone, or metal, which is held in the hand while throwing to assist in shaping the pot or to compact the clay.

RO, R_2O_3, RO_2 The symbols or radicals for the three major groups of chemicals which make up a ceramic glaze. The RO radical refers to the base chemicals, such as the oxides of sodium, potassium, calcium, and lead which function in the glaze as fluxing agents. The R_2O_3 radical refers to the intermediate or amphoteric oxides, some of which may on occasion function either as bases or acids. The chief oxide of interest in this group is alumina (Al_2O_3) which always reacts as a refractory. The third radical RO_2 stands for the acid group which are the glass formers, such as silica (SiO_2).

rouge flambé French, a type of Chinese copper-red reduction glaze (*sang de boeuf*) which is a mottled deep red with green and blue hues, also called a transmutation glaze.

rutile An impure form of titanium dioxide (TiO_2) containing considerable iron. It will give a light yellow or tan color to the glaze with a streaked and runny effect. Used in large amounts it will raise the maturing temperature.

saggars Round boxlike containers of fire clay used in kilns lacking muffles. The glazed ware is placed in saggars to protect the glaze from the combustion gases.

salt glaze A glaze developed by throwing salt ($NaCl$) into a hot kiln. The salt vaporizes and combines with the silica in the body to form sodium silicate, a hard glassy glaze. Today this type of glaze is usually confined to the manufacture of large stoneware crocks and glazed drain tiles. A salt kiln is of a slightly different construction and is limited in use to the salt glaze.

sang de boeuf French, meaning oxblood which describes the rich, deep-red hues produced by the Chinese in their copper-red reduction glazes.

sgraffito Decoration achieved by scratching through a colored slip to show the contrasting body color beneath.

sherd A broken fragment of pottery.

short A body or clay lacking in plasticity.

shrinkage Contraction of the clay in either drying or firing. In the firing cycle the major body shrinkage for stoneware clays begins at approximately 900°C (1652°F). Earthenware clays will begin to fuse and shrink at slightly lower temperatures.

siccative A binding material, such as gum arabic or tragacanth or even Karo sirup, which is added to a glaze to secure a better adhesion to the body. This is especially necessary in fritted glazes containing little or no natural clay.

silica Flint (SiO_2) produced in the United States by grinding almost pure flint sand.

silicate of soda A deflocculant. A standard solution of sodium silicate (commercial N brand) has the ratio of 1 soda to 3.3 silica. Specific gravity 1.395.

single fire A firing cycle in which the normal bisque and glaze firings are combined. The advantages are a great saving of fuel and labor, and development of a stronger bond between the body and glaze. These are partially offset by the need for greater care in handling the ware, and the danger of cracking, if in glazing the raw pieces absorb too much moisture. In a salt glaze, however, these disadvantages do not occur.

sintering A firing process in which ceramic compounds fuse sufficiently to form a solid mass upon cooling, but are not vitrified. An example is low-fired earthenware.

slip A clay in liquid suspension.

slip clay A clay such as Albany and Michigan clays containing sufficient fluxes to function as a glaze with little or no additions.

slip glazes A raw glaze largely composed of plastic clay.

spinel Chemically, magnesium aluminate ($MgAl_2O_3$), an extremely hard crystal arranged in an octahedron atomic structure. In ceramics, a spinel is a colored crystal used as a colorant in place of the metallic oxides because of its greater resistance to change by either the fluxing action of the glaze or the effects of high temperatures.

spray booth A boxlike booth equipped with a ventilating fan to remove spray dust which, whether toxic or not, is harmful.

spraying Applying glazes with a compressed-air-spray machine, the chief commercial method.

sprigging Applying clay in a plastic state to form a relief decoration.

stain Sometimes a single coloring oxide, but usually a combination of oxides, plus alumina, flint, and a fluxing compound. This mixture is calcined and then finely ground and washed. The purpose is to form a stable coloring agent not likely to be altered by the action of the glaze or heat. While stains are employed as glaze colorants, their chief use is as overglaze and underglaze decorations and body colorants.

stilt A ceramic tripod upon which glazed ware is placed in the kiln. Tripods with nickel-nichrome wire points are often used to minimize blemishes to the glaze. They are never used for high-fire porcelain which must be dry footed for greater support.

stoneware A high-fired ware (above cone 8) with a slight or no absorbency. It is usually gray in color but may be tan or slightly reddish. Stoneware is similar in many respects to porcelain, the chief difference being the color which is the result of iron and other impurities in the clay.

stoneware clays Clays more plastic than porcelain, firing above cone 8 to a gray color.

talc ($3MgO \cdot 4SiO_2 \cdot H_2O$) A compound used in most whiteware bodies in the low to moderate firing ranges as a source of silica and flux. It is slightly plastic and may be used to lower the firing range, if need be, of a stoneware or fire-clay body.

terra cotta An earthenware body, generally red in color and containing grog. It is the common type body used for ceramic sculpture.

terra sigillata A sliplike glaze produced during the Etruscan and Greek periods. The finer slip particles were successively decanted off and collected. When applied, burnished, and fired, they gave a glazelike surface. They were not waterproof.

throwing Forming pottery of plastic clay on a potter's wheel.

tin enamel A low-fire opaque glaze originally developed in Persia and carried to Spain by the Moorish conquests. The glaze is lead fluxed, occasionally combined with borax, with tin as an opacifier. The term tin enamel is given to a large body of ware produced in Spain from the eleventh to the fifteenth centuries, as well as the Italian Renaissance pottery, including the glazed terra cottas of della Robbia.

tin-vanadium stain A major yellow colorant produced by a calcined mixture of tin and vanadium oxides.

trailing A method of decorating, using a slip trailed out from a rubber syringe.

translucency The ability of a thin porcelain or whiteware body to transmit a diffused light.

turning Trimming the walls and foot of a pot on the wheel while the clay is in a leather-hard state.

underglaze Colored decoration applied on the bisque ware before the glaze is applied.

viscosity The nonrunning quality of a glaze, caused by glaze chemicals which resist the flowing action of the glaze flux.

vitreous Pertaining to the hard, glassy, and nonabsorbent quality of a body or glaze.

volatilization Action under influence of extreme heat of the kiln in which glaze elements turn successively from a solid to a liquid, and finally into a gaseous, state.

warping Distortion of a pot in drying because of uneven wall thickness or a warm draft of air, or in firing when a kiln does not heat uniformly.

water glass Another term for a liquid solution of sodium silicate which is used as a deflocculant.

ware In general, pottery or porcelain in either the raw, bisque, or glazed state.

water smoking The initial phase of the firing cycle up to a dull red heat (1000° to 1100°F). Depending upon the thickness of the ware, this may take from 2 to 3 hours for thin pottery, to 12 hours for sculpture. The heat rise must be gradual to allow atmospheric and chemical water to escape. In some cases there will be vegetable impurities which will also burn out, releasing carbon monoxide.

wax resist A method of decorating pottery by brushing on a design with a warm wax solution or a wax emulsion. This will prevent an applied stain or glaze from adhering to the decorated portions. The wax may be applied to either the raw or bisque ware or between two layers of glaze.

weathering Generally the exposure of raw clay to the action of rain, sun, and freezing weather which breaks down the particle size and renders the clay more plastic.

wedging Kneading and cutting plastic clay, forcibly throwing down one piece upon the other in order to obtain a uniform texture free from air pockets.

white lead [$2PbCO_3 \cdot Pb(OH)_2$] A major low-fire flux.

whiteware Pottery or chinaware with a white or light-cream colored body.

whiting Calcium carbonate ($CaCO_2$), similar chemically to limestone and marble; a major high-fire flux.

yellow base A glaze stain produced by a calcined mixture of red lead, antimony, and tin oxides.

zircopax A commercial frit used as an opacifier. It is composed of zirconium oxide, tin oxide, and silica. It gives less of a tint than tin oxide, but its price is considerably lower.

INDEX

INDEX

For ceramic terms, see Glossary, pp. 218-227. For ceramic chemicals, see pp. 129-143.

EXPERIMENTAL GLAZE NOTES

EXPERIMENTAL GLAZE NOTES